The Middle Voice

THE MIDDLE VOICE

Mediating Conflict Successfully

SECOND EDITION

Joseph B. Stulberg
and
Lela P. Love

CAROLINA ACADEMIC PRESS
Durham, North Carolina

Library of Congress Cataloging-in-Publication Data

Stulberg, Joseph B.
  [Taking charge/managing conflict]
  The middle voice : mediating conflict successfully / Joseph B.
Stulberg and Lela P. Love. -- Second edition.
      pages cm
  Updated and expanded version of the author's Taking charge/managing
conflict, c1987.
  ISBN 978-1-61163-408-2 (alk. paper)
  1. Conflict management. 2. Mediation. I. Love, Lela Porter, 1950- II. Title.

HD42.S78 2012
658.4'053--dc23

                    2012042112

                    CAROLINA ACADEMIC PRESS
                    700 Kent Street
              Durham, North Carolina 27701
                Telephone (919) 489-7486
                    Fax (919) 493-5668
                    www.cap-press.com
            Printed in the United States of America

For my wife, Midge, and my children, Jonathan, Michael, Gita, Charles and Heather, who have been unwavering in their support of my interest and activities in conflict resolution—and much beyond. My life has been wonderful because they are central to it. JBS

For my family, Peter and Nicole, who have provided a nucleus of intense energy, inspiration and love. Their presence and support have kept this—and every other—endeavor vital. LPL

Contents

Map of *The Middle Voice*

Preface to the Second Edition

THE MIDDLE VOICE

We live in a connected world.

Thanks to extraordinary technological advances in transportation and communication, we can readily interact with persons from throughout the world who embrace living habits and speak languages that differ from our own. Those differences are instantly visible or apparent to us.

But we do not need to travel the world, either physically or electronically, to encounter differences. Each of us grows up as a member of an identifiable general culture. And as we live our lives, our personal identity becomes woven with and enriched by the distinctive practices of other groups of which we become members, be they professional, recreational, religious, or geographical. Medical doctors have their own cultural norms, as do bikers or movie actors or political activists; and the list goes on.

On many occasions, when people engage in conduct that generates misunderstanding and conflicts, their actions are importantly shaped by the distinctive practices and values of their various identity groups. Whether a dispute involves allegations of human rights abuses, a failed commercial business venture, or the sounds of an apparently non-stop fiesta celebration at the house of one's next door neighbor, if a mediator wants to help those disputing parties better understand their concerns, identify multiple ways to address them, and generate mutually acceptable resolutions, then he must be acutely attuned to how the backgrounds, practices and beliefs of all participants in the mediation conference, including his own, impact the process.

In this second edition of The Middle Voice, we try, in a new Chapter 12, to explicitly identify the challenges that human diversity dynamics present to a mediator for constructively dealing with differences, and how a mediator, using the BADGER framework presented in (newly reorganized) Part III, can thoughtfully and effectively embrace them.

Except for corrections for typographical or grammatical errors, all other aspects of the first edition remain unchanged.

We remain deeply grateful to the many people from multiple countries that have shared with us their enthusiastic reaction to this text. We continue to enrich our own understanding of, and love for, this activity by their thoughtful suggestions. More important, their excitement about, and appropriate confidence in, using these mediation skills in settings ranging from mediating multiparty public policy disputes to controversies among co-workers at the worksite or among volunteer Board members of a not-for-profit agency reaffirms for us that mediating skills are importantly useful—and deployed—in multiple settings in our lives. And that mediating well is a richly rewarding human experience for each of us.

JBS
LPL
January 2013

Acknowledgments

In 1987, Josh Stulberg wrote *Taking Charge/Managing Conflict*. This book updates and expands it in several important ways.

For twenty five years, we have used the framework outlined in *The Middle Voice* when conducting mediator training programs—at both the beginning and advanced levels—for lawyer/mediators in court-annexed mediation programs, public officials serving in governmental agencies, leaders and volunteers of community organizations, and students in universities throughout the United States and Western, Central and Eastern Europe. This book considerably enriches the first version as a result of wonderful, helpful feedback from students and training participants, as well as our own enhanced understanding both from teaching and from mediating.

The field of "dispute resolution" and, with it, the practice and challenges of mediating, have changed importantly since the publication of the first edition of this book. "Mediating" is part of today's normal vocabulary—people, as citizens, family members, or participants at the workplace often "participate" in mediation sessions. The most notable changes are institutional and civic. Institutionally, the use of mediation in the United States to resolve court-annexed civil litigation of all kinds has grown exponentially, and its use by private organizations and governmental agencies to address employer-employee, interagency, or agency-citizen conflicts has seen comparable expansion. At the civic level, the design, values and implementation of mediating processes in emerging democracies, from countries in Central and Eastern Europe to those in the Far East, has become a central component of democracy-building efforts. In our view, these exciting developments require both a sharpened understanding of the basic values and goals of the mediation process—and its impact on mediator strategies—and a searching examination of how the process can and should adapt to new settings. We hope this text meets those challenges.

Many persons have helped enrich our understanding of the mediation process. Stand outs are Robert A. Baruch Bush, James Coben, Nancy H. Rogers, the late Raymond Shonholtz, Andrew Thomas, Sharon Press and Dan Weitz. By their examples, they have taught us more about mediating than they could possibly know. Roger Deitz's attention to and persistence in editing improved this manuscript. To all these stars, and our other wonderful colleagues in dispute resolution, we are most grateful.

Part 1

Responses to Conflict

1

The Middle Voice

Society's greatest opportunities . . . lie in tapping . . . human inclinations toward collaboration and compromise rather than stirring our proclivities for competition and rivalry.

Derek Bok

The scenes are familiar.

Employees threaten to strike for higher wages. College students disrupt classes and take over university buildings to advocate hiring minority faculty and transforming the curriculum to make it more globally sensitive. Parents converge on a school board meeting to demand repeal of its decision to close their neighborhood school. Discussions become shouting matches. Tempers flare.

Suddenly, doors shut. A mediator is meeting with the disputing parties. A statement is expected at the conclusion of their talks. Soon the parties emerge. They are talking to each other and report that they have resolved their differences. Their controversy has evaporated into a resolution.

What happened? What did the mediator do that enabled those persons who had been entangled in controversy to resolve their differences?

Successful mediators are skilled at forging common ground among disputants. In a deliberate, conscious way, they prompt persons to clarify interests and transform rhetoric into proposals. They urge persons to establish priorities and consider trade-offs. They help disputants to develop settlement options that are tempered by political, legal, or resource constraints.

Mediators explore the significance of what is said and what is not said. They highlight inconsistencies and vulnerabilities to generate flexibility and develop a framework for agreement.

Succinctly stated, mediators manage a dispute resolution process. Managing it effectively is no accident. Mediators embrace distinctive values, develop critical skills, perform specific tasks, adhere to precise language practices, and use proven settlement-building strategies. These values and practices define the mediator's role. They can be identified and taught. Once learned, people can use them consciously and repeatedly when assisting others in resolving disputes.

All of us use mediation skills and strategies. Life demands them again and again. For example:

- A CEO dispatches a special assistant to meet with two company division presidents whose respective divisions market competing, non-compatible products to the same customer. His[1] task is to help the division presidents negotiate acceptable guidelines that sustain intracorporate independence and competition without unreasonably jeopardizing the continuing business relationship with valued customers.
- A parent interrupts his children's heated argument over what television program they will watch at 8:00 P.M. and assists them to discuss an acceptable plan.
- A teacher gets two groups of shouting students to agree on how they will share the school's basketball court during the lunch hour.
- Members of a community organization ask one of its most distinguished citizens to play peacemaker among competing factions of the board of directors.

Conflict is inescapable. In some roles, we find ourselves helping others resolve their disputes. That is what a mediator does. The question is not whether we will mediate. The question is: How well will we do it?

---

[1] We have alternated the use of male and female gender by chapters.

2

Intervener Models

People fail to get along because they fear each other; they fear each other because they don't know each other; they don't know each other because they have not communicated with each other.

Martin Luther King, Jr.

Mediation is a process in which a neutral intervener helps people in a dispute improve their understanding of their situation and one another and then develop solutions that are acceptable to them. Unlike a judge or an arbitrator, the mediator has no authority to impose a binding decision on the disputants. The mediator can only persuade them to work things out.

There are many types of interveners who help persons resolve conflicts. A personnel director helps a supervisor and a subordinate resolve performance problems stemming from racial or ethnic bias. A city ombudsperson investigates citizen complaints against a public agency and seeks responses that will satisfy all concerned. A good samaritan breaks up a shouting match among teenagers in a public park and gets them to agree not to disturb each other.

But not all interveners are mediators. What distinguishes a mediator is the duty, both personally and institutionally, to be neutral. That means operating without any preference for resolving the controversy in a particular way. Commitment to rules and standards on the one hand, or, to party choice, on the other, will determine the type of intervener.

This difference is crucial. When we distinguish intervener roles on the basis of whether the intervener has a duty to enforce independently established rules and standards or is neutral and committed to promoting party self-determination, two distinct models emerge: the compliance officer and the coach.

The Compliance Officer

Some interveners help disputing parties reach an agreement only if that agreement is compatible with corporate, institutional or public rules. If settlement terms violate those norms, then the intervener must veto their consideration even if all parties find them acceptable.

Consider the trivial case of a corporate dress code. A subordinate violates the "business casual" dress code policy that prohibits wearing jeans and, for men, collarless shirts. When her supervisor disciplines her, the subordinate appeals to an employee counselor to help them work out "a mutually satisfactory arrangement." The counselor can focus discussion on the propriety of the discipline but not on whether the rule is wise or desirable. The counselor cannot permit the supervisor and the subordinate to make an exception to the rule even if the supervisor now asserts being agreeable to doing so. Even if the counselor believes the rule is silly, she cannot join the quiet conspiracy to junk it. She must either change the rule through established procedures or change jobs.

The more rules there are, the less chance there is for the intervener to be neutral in any meaningful sense. In disputes subject to a rule's application, one's responsibility as an intervener is straightforward: persuade the people to comply with the governing rules.

The Coach

Some interveners act as a catalyst to help disputants understand their predicament and resolve their concerns on terms acceptable to them, regardless of the intervener's opinion of the agreement. The coach helps manage interactions, spot opportunities for collaboration, and assist parties develop new paths to address the issues. The result, though, always is an outcome that all parties endorse.

There are two exceptions to this standard that the disputants' preferences are decisive. First, an intervener must have some confidence that the parties are competent to bargain. A person who is visibly drunk or clinically depressed might not be able to understand her own interests or make meaningful commitments. A victim of domestic violence, frightened of her abuser and unwilling to say anything to provoke him, is not able to bargain—at least not without protections in place. In other words, the "agreement" of such persons might be illusory. In many practice contexts, such cases are screened prior to mediation in order to assess party competency. Further, during mediated discussions, a skillful mediator can uncover dynamics indicating lack of competency. In either situation, parties are either provided with assistance to insure competent participation or referred to a different process.

Second, settlement terms must be legal. If a store owner fires an employee but later offers to rehire that person "off the books" so both can avoid paying taxes, the intervener's duty as a citizen would prevent endorsing such unlawful conduct even if the employee found the proposed arrangement acceptable. In most situations, though, people don't typically parade their willingness to engage in illegal conduct before a mediator.

For most conflicts, whether involving a landlord and tenant disputing about back rent or siblings fighting about the division of their parent's estate, the parties are competent and free to design solutions they find acceptable. The coach's role is to encourage, facilitate, and manage the discussion and resolution process.

A mediator is a coach who consistently and persistently prompts disputing parties to understand one another and develop mutually acceptable options. Contrasted with discussions facilitated by an intervener as compliance officer targeted at securing compliance with a rule, a mediated discussion can be an instrument for change. Customs, practices, laws, and values change over time, and individuals can prompt change as well as adjust to it. Unlike a compliance officer, a mediator helps develop new approaches and strategies to address a situation. She assumes that no conventional practice is immutable, no topic ineligible for discussion and no mandatory standards dictate the acceptability of settlement terms. This does not mean that everything is possible in a practical sense, but that reality represents an annoying practical problem rather than an impenetrable constraint. How does this work in practice?

Suppose a group of parents demand that school officials reduce the athletic budget and use the excess funds to purchase microcomputers for classroom use. The parents demonstrate in front of the high school to press their demand. Nothing would prevent an intervener from having the school officials and protesting parents discuss this matter. Nothing need stop them from reaching an agreement, even if that agreement could not be implemented immediately because of existing contractual obligations with the teachers' union. All that the parties must acknowledge is that implementing their agreement requires additional collaboration with—and possibly amendment by—other constituencies.

This simple lesson bears repeating: practices and policies can be changed if people commit themselves to persevering through the discussion process. Advocating and securing change through discussion and persuasion is one of the principal nonviolent change-making procedures of a democratic society. Using a mediator to manage such discussions can develop the momentum and direction that enable such talks to succeed.

Thus a mediator is a neutral intervener who operates as a coach, not as a compliance officer. She enjoys enormous freedom in prodding disputants to pay attention to each other's interests and to consider a range of possible settlement options. Although an individual's own values might lead to refusing to serve as mediator in certain disputes, a person must acknowledge that power and effectiveness as a mediator emanate from a steadfast commitment to neutrality— to helping the parties develop settlement terms that they find acceptable, even if the mediator finds those terms objectionable.

It is easy to state that the parties' preferences should prevail. It is much harder to act according to that precept. Most of us like to give orders. In our various roles as friends, co-workers, supervisors, parents, colleagues, group members, or citizens, we are always ready to dispense advice.

Mediating, however, demands that we shed our authoritarian and paternalistic instincts. It compels us to take seriously our commitment to democratic decision-making in our homes, schools, businesses, and communities. We pay a price for using such a process: people sometimes make mistakes, cater to greed, or act expediently. But to those who cherish freedom, the alternatives to mediated discussions are even less attractive.

Thus the challenge remains: How well will we mediate?

3

Patterns in Conflict: Perceptions, Parties, Problems, Processes, Principles and Practicalities

Two roads diverged in a wood, and I, I took the one less traveled by, and that has made all the difference.

Robert Frost

What is a mediator getting into upon agreeing to serve? Although the atmosphere and the issues differ in each dispute, there are patterns common to all controversies. The Chinese characters for the word "crisis"—危机—represent danger and opportunity. Most conflicts have elements of danger—the emotions of each party, clashing positions, and polarized views of the other side. But they also contain building blocks for progress—opportunities to create new paths of interaction and accommodation. Most people are acutely aware of the first dimension. A mediator focuses on both, working vigorously to help parties overcome the dangers and capitalize on the opportunities.

Perceptions

What is the first thing that comes to mind upon hearing the word *conflict*? Typical responses are captured in the chart on the next page. These words highlight a crucial observation: our images about being in conflict regularly reflect negative feelings. Most people do not describe disputes as opportunities for personal growth or intellectual challenge. Rarely do they associate positive attitudes or beliefs, like excitement, stimulation, or resolution, with their image of *conflict*. Quite the contrary. While the intensity of feelings varies with the particular circumstances, most of us feel, quite understandably, as though any dispute in which we are involved has only costs: emotional, financial, or social. We rarely perceive any benefits from being embroiled in a dispute. We consider a dispute to be an aberration from the more desirable state of harmony. If we were describing an ideal world, most of us would not include disputes as part of it.

This widespread way of thinking about disputes has a significant impact on how we approach resolving them. How do we resolve a situation that gives rise to anxiety, frustration, stress, or grief? *By eliminating the source of these negative feelings.* Anything short of that often seems an undesirable compromise.

But acting on that impulse, though understandable, is utterly impractical. Suppose your neighbor's dog barks all night, making it impossible to sleep. Shooting the dog or forcing the neighbor to move is not a viable solution. If a ten-year-old disagrees with his parents about watching a violent movie on television, the child leaving home or the parents throwing him out are options—but probably not good ones. An employee does not quit a job simply because a co-worker refuses to retract a stinging criticism. In such situations, some option other than elimination is needed.

Although eliminating the source of the controversy is usually impractical, the desire to do so is real. Some dispute resolution processes constrain that emotion more than others. Fighting permits an emotional and physical melee to develop, but fighting in a courtroom invites a contempt citation. Every mediator must appreciate the intensity of these antagonistic feelings and develop guidelines for addressing them. The challenge can be stated simply: How can the mediator reorient the way disputants see their conflict and each other so that they view a developed solution that does not involve anyone's annihilation or capitulation as a desirable outcome rather than a poor second choice?

Parties

Who becomes entangled in disputes? The answer is simple: each of us, either individually or as an institutional member. Unless we are hermits, we will have disputes with family and friends, with co-workers, with professionals we retain, with teachers or counselors who work with our children, as a landlord or a tenant, or as a citizen interacting with the government. We will probably have disputes with strangers we encounter on buses and in stores. A sports team, club, or college will have disputes with other institutions. A country has disputes with other countries.

This list of parties, of course, is incomplete. It is sufficient, however, to remind us that:

- Anyone can be in a dispute. Good or bad, wise or foolish—no one escapes conflict.
- Everyone must meet the challenge of dealing with conflict or pay the consequences for failure.

Problems

What kinds of problems give rise to disputes? Disputes occur over everything: rent and repairs, parenting arrangements, purchasing property, building construction delays, business partnerships, drawing borders between countries, harsh comments, where to eat dinner, and the amount of damages for injuries sustained in an accident. The list is endless, and reminds us that:

- Disputes occur frequently, not just occasionally; they are part of everyday living.
- Disputes differ in terms of intensity, complexity and importance.

Processes

Most of us resolve our disputes. It is a destructive myth to think that disputes are inherently unsolvable. How well we do so is another matter.

How do we resolve disputes? We are incredibly resourceful in finding ways. Well known processes include: litigation,[1] arbitration,[2] mediation[3] and negotiation.[4] However, the list of practices and processes we regularly use to address conflicts is much broader. People in disputes might: avoid, delay, take drugs, drink, sleep, study the situation, give in, create a committee or task force, get advice, stonewall, consult an expert, split the difference, talk, yell, vote, legislate, boycott, demonstrate, write a letter, get an elder to help, offer a bribe, lie, cheat, allow someone else to decide, flip a coin, use extortion or coercion, make "an offer that can't be refused," or go to war. And this is only a partial list.

The availability of alternatives means that voluntary processes like negotiation and mediation are fragile. Angry or disappointed parties can stop participating whenever they want and for whatever reason they choose.

Just because we use various options does not mean that they are effective or that we approve of their use. The basis on which we select the process or combination of processes will be discussed later. First we must emphasize how mediation differs from other methods.

Popular media most often show four ways of resolving conflict: fighting, voting, litigating, and complying with a decision made by the person "with authority." These methods share two essential characteristics: first, someone must win while others lose; second, except in the case of fighting, it is assumed that everyone accepts the process and agrees to abide by its outcome, even if the result is unfavorable. We assume, for instance, that subordinates will implement their superior's directives, losing parties in a lawsuit will comply with

---

[1] Litigation is a public dispute resolution process where parties communicate complaints alleged to violate legal rights and initiate procedures designed to seek redress pursuant to publicly promulgated, posted laws and rules.

[2] Arbitration is a private and voluntary dispute resolution process where parties agree to submit their dispute for binding resolution to a party-chosen third party neutral.

[3] Mediation is a private and voluntary dispute resolution process where the parties agree that a party-chosen neutral intervener (the mediator) will help them identify issues of concern, develop options responsive to the issues, and find a resolution acceptable to all parties.

[4] Negotiation is a voluntary process where parties identify issues of concern, develop options responsive to the issues, and attempt to find a resolution acceptable to all parties.

the judge's decision—at least after all appeals are exhausted—, and that the losers of an election will abide by the election results. But we all know that life does not always work so neatly.

Mediation differs from these methods on both of these fundamental points: it protects people from losing because each participant can veto a proposed solution, and it increases the probability that those involved will comply with the outcome by requiring those affected by the dispute to participate in developing solutions for it. Conceptually speaking, mediation is a dramatic departure from these well-known processes because it makes us think strategically about how to persuade, not force, others to do what we want them to do. It requires us to treat people differently because we must convince them to cooperate with us in order to achieve our own goals. In practice, we use mediation techniques more frequently than we use these other procedures. Life demands it.

Principles

Why do we choose some processes over others for resolving certain disputes? On what basis, for example, do we choose to ignore rather than litigate a supervisor's denial of our request to take vacation time during August? Why don't we approve of letting high school students fight to resolve arguments that arise from relentless teasing or sexist name-calling? Should we decide the location of toxic waste sites by public vote, legislation, or the forces of the market?

These are not idle questions for the intellectually curious. Each time we resolve a dispute, we are choosing a particular dispute settlement process or combination of processes. In making that choice, we automatically give an answer—perhaps a controversial one—to this important query.

We can answer the fundamental question in two steps. First, we must develop a set of standards for evaluating each dispute resolution process. Such standards include the following:

1. *Publicity.* The public (or private) nature of the process.
2. *Precedent.* The precedents set both by the use of the process and by its results.
3. *Efficiency.* Cost in time, money and emotional or psychological stress of the process used.
4. *Outcome.* The wisdom of the results both in meeting parties' interests and comporting with social norms.
5. *Participation.* The degree of participation in the dispute resolution process by those who must live with its results.

6. *Relationships.* The impact of using the dispute resolution process on the relationship among the disputing parties.
7. *Compliance and Durability.* Whether the outcome reached reflects do-able and durable arrangements.
8. *Fairness.* The fairness and justice of the process used.

We then measure each process against these criteria. For example, *giving in* presumably consumes insignificant resources in terms of time and money, so it scores high on efficiency. But *giving in* certainly does not guarantee a wise outcome to a conflict or a fair process; hence the process scores low on those criteria.

After going through this empirical analysis for each process, we proceed to the second, and more difficult, step. We must now rank criteria in the order of their importance. Doing that requires that we apply fundamental principles of our morality: our belief in freedom of thought and expression, our commitment to treat others with equal respect and dignity, our willingness to constrain our liberty of action by considerations of fair play and integrity, and our interest in social order or economic growth. Once we decide which principle is most important to us in a given situation, we can determine which standard—efficiency, participation in the decision-making process, fairness, and so forth—shall be decisive. Then, drawing on the results of our empirical analysis in the first step, we choose the particular dispute resolution process.

> *Example 1.* An employee believes that his corporation's accounting practices violate the law by understating the company's future liability for pension benefits. His supervisor, the vice-president in charge of finance, heatedly disputes the employee's analysis. How do they resolve this dispute? They may consult with other colleagues, or perhaps hire an outside consultant for expert advice. Typically, an employee does not immediately "blow the whistle" by contacting the government. First, he tries to resolve the dispute through internal channels. Why? Principles of loyalty, affection, and responsibilities of individual group members toward one another compel an employee to choose a dispute resolution process—negotiation—that ranks high on the criterion of not irreparably damaging the continuing working relationship of the disputants.

> *Example 2.* The decision to build a nuclear power plant affects many people. It also generates many disputes regarding location, size, and safety features, all of which dramatically affect the distribution of

benefits and burdens among citizens and businesses alike. Our conception of a desirable political and economic community requires that we treat everyone with equal respect; that fairness commitment prompts us to resolve these disputes in a way that ensures broad-based participation and public discussion, even at the expense of economic efficiency. Thus we often choose to resolve controversies over such issues through the legislative and judicial processes rather than through private negotiation.

So we must restate the obvious. On the basis of a considered analysis of our fundamental values—moral, religious, political, and economic—we determine priorities among those standards against which we will evaluate dispute resolution processes. We then select a specific process for resolving a particular dispute in light of the empirical data that demonstrate how well that process operates according to the standards we have judged to be most important. Thus, each time we use a particular process to resolve a dispute, *no matter what the substantive outcome might be*, we make a statement about the values we cherish and the type of people we want to be.

How do these comments relate to mediators and the mediation process? If we recommend mediation to resolve a dispute, we must do so by answering the questions posed here. Hence we must understand the strengths and weaknesses of mediation by evaluating it according to the standards noted and identifying the broader values and principles that support its choice.

Mediation is private. Privacy invites candid communication and deflates public posturing, thereby promoting reduced hostility and improved understanding and relationships. At the same time, the lack of publicity means that the public cannot monitor whether social justice concerns are being met in individual cases.

The precedential value of an agreement reached through mediation is limited. It does not usually become a public and binding legal precedent like a litigated outcome. Its terms reflect only the preferences and priorities of the particular parties involved, rather than being a statement about public norms. However, the precedential value of using mediation to resolve certain types of disputes is strong because its use acknowledges that all parties have concerns that must be addressed and that parties are capable of finding a resolution themselves. Also, a good outcome—broadcast informally—can be copied by others in similar situations.

Mediated discussions can take time to conclude. Sometimes no agreement or resolution is reached. Hence, mediation is not always efficient. However, its informal nature minimizes both administrative costs and the participants' financial costs. And often mediation can bring a speedy closure to conflict.

Substantively, mediated discussions result in better understanding among the parties and, given that mediators urge parties to choose thoughtfully from among many developed options, mediated results often reflect creative outcomes tailored to serve the parties' particular interests. Mediation provides no assurance, however, that public norms will be embraced, as the parties can develop norms that comport with their own values.

Mediation requires the disputants to assume the major responsibility for resolving their conflict. Self-determination and outcome control impact parties' participation and relationship, as well as the durability of the resolution.

The mediator's presence deters unilateral attempts to skew the ground rules in one side's favor or otherwise violate basic due process requirements, thereby enhancing procedural fairness. The parties' endorsement of the outcome hopefully reflects their belief that the resolution was fair.

Thus, mediation ranks at the lower end of the spectrum on the first two standards (publicity and precedent), as it is a private process and sets no public precedent. With respect to the third and fourth standards (efficiency and outcome) the results are mixed: using mediation may efficiently resolve the dispute, but its use might also be an expensive, failed effort. Mediation might achieve a creative outcome, optimal for the particular parties; at the same time, the outcome might violate social norms. On the remaining standards—participation, relationships, compliance and durability, and fairness—mediation fares exceedingly well.

To complete the second step of the analysis, we must identify those values that support our choice to use mediation rather than another dispute settlement process. Mediation embraces the principle of equality—that each person be treated with equal dignity and respect. Its commitment to democratic decision-making and self-determination provides a bulwark against paternalism, authoritarianism, and violence dominating the decision-making process. Mediation ensures that each decision maker counts as one and no more than one. It ensures that the decision-makers are those directly affected by the outcome, not kings, technocrats or those with the largest arsenal of weapons.

From a moral perspective, mediation makes individuals assume personal responsibility for their conduct. It develops enriched interaction with others, and successful mediation promotes community bonds through increased communication and restored trust.

Finally, mediation supports flexibility and creativity. It encourages disputants to blend the lessons of their own human experience into shaping solutions to the problems they identify. This, in turn, builds individual and social capacity to solve problems and work collaboratively.

These values constitute the core of the democratic way of life. They are constitutive of the mediation process. Mediation is not a radical process, but it is unusual in that it takes very seriously the rhetoric that all persons affected by a controversy should be included as equal decision-makers in resolving it.

Practicalities

If mediation is so good, why don't people insist on using it all the time? Skeptics offer different views on what "really" motivates people to resolve disputes the way they do:

1. *Power*: Those with power use any process that advances their agenda. If you don't have power, you must dance to the tune of those that do.

2. *Self-interest.* People choose the dispute resolution process that they believe will enable them to prevail. Talk about participation, relationships and fairness in the process is nonsense. People act to further their self-interest. If someone expects to win a lawsuit, he will sue; if he thinks he might lose, he will consider other options.

3. *Psychological Distortions and Strategic Posturing.* People feel their situation is different from situations where mediation works. In the familiar process of demonizing the other side, parties often react negatively to any association or proposal related to their adversary. They are overconfident about their own stance. They do not want to feel vulnerable by opening up to the other side or signaling a willingness to compromise.

4. *Self-protection.* A savvy person does not put all eggs in one basket. Rather than only using mediation, he might deploy a combination of dispute settlement processes, moving from one to another as his interests dictate.

The skeptics warn us not to be naive about these elements of human behavior when trying to resolve disputes. But they overstate their case.

Power

It is true that people who have the unilateral power to get what they want have no need for mediation. Indeed, they have no need for anyone; they should simply do whatever they must in order to achieve their goals. But it is extremely rare that anyone has this much one-sided power. Abused children can get police assistance. Corporate presidents need shareholder approval and subordinate co-operation to achieve their stated objectives. And the list goes on.

No one denies that in particular circumstances some individuals have more power than others. A boss often has more power than his subordinate over the latter's continued employment status; the young woman living in the upstairs apartment has the power to disrupt her downstairs neighbor's peace and quiet by playing drums at 2:00 a.m.; and the teacher has the power to affect a student's academic success. But the skeptics jump from acknowledging those realities to concluding that the victim has *no* power. That is just not so. Some people may act as though they are both infallible and invincible, but we are all vulnerable in some ways. In appropriate circumstances, the employee can challenge his boss by filing a grievance, speaking to a superior, or starting a lawsuit. The apartment dweller can complain constantly to the landlord. The student can spread damaging rumors about the teacher. Whether people recognize that they have power—or, more important, have the desire and courage to use it—are separate considerations that have very practical consequences. Most of us have some power in all situations, and the power dynamics between individuals shift as different issues arise and new circumstances come into play.

Self-Interest

The insight that people and groups choose processes that promote their self-interest is meaningless until we define *self-interest*; once we do so, the "insight" is no longer useful.

Suppose, for example, that a tenant has fallen behind in her rent payments by two months. When the landlord asks about the rent, the tenant reminds him of an earlier conversation in which the tenant informed the landlord that the kitchen appliances were not working and that rent would be paid only when repairs were made. The landlord decides to consult you. He defines his self-interest as "getting as much money as possible from the tenant" and asks for advice about which dispute resolution process to use. What would you advise? You would not say "Do whatever promotes your self-interest"—that would leave the landlord with no better idea of what to do than before he asked you for help. But you could help him by identifying the possible outcomes of using competing dispute resolution processes, thereby forcing him to define his "self-interest."

For instance, you might point out that he might win the largest monetary award by suing the tenant, but he would have to reduce that award by money spent on attorney's fees and advertising for a new tenant, as well as any rent lost by having the apartment vacant until a new tenant is found. An alternative would be to engage promptly in mediated discussions and press for a settlement that minimally recoups some of the rent in return for promptly fixing the appliances.

What does the landlord mean by "getting as much money as possible from the tenant"—getting the highest total dollar amount from the tenant regardless of the costs incurred to obtain it, or getting the highest *net* amount from the tenant? The landlord must assess the strengths and weaknesses of each dispute resolution process to identify her preferred outcomes or components of self-interest; then he can choose to use the procedure most likely to secure them.

Psychological Distortions and Strategic Posturing

Many disputants see one another as unreasonable and conclude that it may be pointless to work with an unreasonable person. Experiencing self-righteous anger, disputants want a judge to proclaim them right and are overconfident about their chances for success. Suggestions from the other side—including a proposal to mediate—are viewed skeptically. Mediation, however, can work even though disputants begin with little esteem or trust for one another and little hope that mediation can succeed. Mediation is an excellent forum to test whether perceptions are in fact distorted and to gain an appreciation of the other side.

In addition to psychological distortions, parties often adopt competitive strategies that make mediation seem unworkable. For example, parties might take extreme and inflexible positions and refuse to share information with one another about their real interests. In such circumstances, it is logical to think mediation will be fruitless. Nonetheless, a skilled mediator, using such tools as private meetings, will be able to see where movement is possible and guide parties accordingly.

These cited reasons *not* to mediate are points that make the intervention of a skilled mediator particularly useful.

Self-protection

The skeptics note, correctly, that people often use several dispute resolution processes simultaneously. Those who oppose the construction of a new federal highway might attempt to block its development by initiating court action, while simultaneously conducting a sit-in at the proposed site, picketing city hall, and offering to participate in professionally mediated discussions with various government officials and private developers to try to reach a resolution. Lawyers often initiate a lawsuit on behalf of their clients but then negotiate a settlement "on the courthouse steps" just before the trial.

But the skeptics have paid less attention to the way in which using one process can distort or undermine the use of others. Let's consider an obvious foul-up: state officials agree to meet at 3:00 p.m. with a group of prisoners who are holding prison guards as hostages; simultaneously, they order state police officers to storm the prison beginning at 3:00 p.m., using whatever force is necessary to quash the uprising. Although some might applaud the use of the negotiating session as a decoy, clearly both processes cannot genuinely operate at the same time. Other examples indicate that we can operate at cross-purposes in far more subtle ways.

Suppose a couple decides to divorce; they have two children, ages five and seven. How should they settle their differences with respect to dividing their property, caring for the children, and assuming financial obligations? If one party, say the wife, initiates a lawsuit, the other party must respond or jeopardize his legal posture. Assume the wife, or her lawyer, then suggests to the husband, or his lawyer, that they try to negotiate a settlement. But a new dynamic has now entered the negotiation process. The husband is a party to a lawsuit. He may be cautious about considering any settlement option that might force him to share information that could be damaging in subsequent litigation.

The posturing that accompanies the assertion of legal rights escalates the tension and bitterness among the disputants, thereby undermining the constructive future relationship that the negotiation process, when operating alone, is designed to promote. By placing the negotiations within the framework of a lawsuit, one potentially undermines the problem-solving spirit so essential to effective negotiations. Getting an agreement in such circumstances is not impossible, but it is normally more difficult. The dynamic among the parties would be significantly different if they committed themselves to trying to resolve their differences through joint discussions for a specified time period and initiating litigation only if such efforts failed.

We operate in a complex world. No dispute resolution process operates in a vacuum. We often use several processes simultaneously to signal to others that we are serious about our aspirations and expect to be treated accordingly. Having acknowledged that, however, we must make certain the strategy does not backfire. We must ensure that simultaneous use does not diminish the processes' distinctive strengths.

Mediation is not a panacea, but it is a remarkably effective process for resolving a wide range of controversies—from those among co-workers or quarreling siblings to those among nations trying to secure the peaceable exchange of political prisoners.

Successful mediation is not an accident. A mediator does more than just "use common sense." He acts in deliberate, thoughtful, and structured ways to try to promote understanding and agreements. No mediator can ever guarantee a successful outcome, but he will not stop trying to create one until he has exhausted every available strategy. In Part II we examine the mediator's job and how he sets the stage for a successful process, and in Part III we examine the elements of successful mediation efforts.

Part 2

Setting the Stage

4

The Mediator's Job

Do you have the patience to wait
till your mud settles and the water is clear?
Can you remain unmoving
till the right action arises by itself?
                    Tao te Ching 15 (Steven Mitchell trans., 1991)

The mediator's job is to get negotiating parties to understand themselves better, understand one another better, develop options to address the disputed issues, and agree to terms that resolve their controversy. We must identify the specific responsibilities that define this job and those personal qualities that enable the mediator to execute these tasks.

Job Description of a Mediator

The mediator has primary responsibility for structuring and managing discussions directed at achieving enhanced understanding and mutually acceptable solutions to the issues in dispute. These functions are both procedural and substantive.

Chairperson

The mediator must create a well-structured meeting that is also comfortable and safe. Working with the parties and their representatives, she is responsible for scheduling the number, time, and place of meetings, for establishing the format of each meeting and the number of persons who participate, and for arranging for making computer, photocopying, telephone, and other support services available for the parties. Substantively, the mediator is responsible for focusing the discussion, controlling participant behavior, and sustaining a positive conversational dynamic. A mediator performs this function in every dispute, although the extent to which it applies varies with the situation.

> *Examples.* A teacher who tries to resolve a dispute between two students who are throwing food at each other in a school cafeteria does not have to worry about scheduling meetings or providing clerical services to the disputants. She need only direct the discussions between them. She must create some format or environment in which the students can effectively deal with each other rather than let them stand at opposite ends of the room and shout at each other in front of their classmates.
>
> A person who mediates a dispute between a landlord and a tenant organization while a rent strike is in progress, however, must consider such matters as where to meet, who should be present, and the scheduling of multiple meetings.

Communicator

Parties to a dispute often do not listen to or understand what others are saying. The mediator must transmit ideas, positions, convictions, and emotions in such a way that they understand each other. Mediators must also realize that people frequently communicate indirectly.

> *Example.* Lopez vehemently accuses a neighbor, Jones, of kicking her in the shins, but then focuses the rest of the discussion on the concern that Jones's dog comes onto Lopez's property, overturns the garbage can, and scatters the garbage all over the yard. Lopez has communicated some very important information—namely, that the concern about the alleged assault and battery pales in significance next to her desire to control the dog's behavior. The mediator must make certain that Jones understands Lopez's priorities so that discussion is appropriately focused.

Parties sometimes fail to reach agreement not because what is said is objectionable but because the language in which statements and proposals are couched triggers fear or another negative response. The mediator's function in such a situation is to reframe communications into language that increases the probability of a favorable reception. The mediator never camouflages or eliminates information when translating; the task is to reduce the sting of ill-chosen words.

> *Examples.* When talking with management, a mediator reframes a union proposal for a $4.50/hour wage increase as a wage proposal of 3 percent. Similarly, a mediator translates a neighbor's proposal that the seventeen-year-old not play her sound system or television from 11:00 p.m. until 7:00 a.m. each night as an offer that she *can* play those systems seven days a week from 7:00 a.m. until 11:00 p.m.—sixteen hours a day!

Educator

The mediator must empathize with the aspirations of the parties and understand the technical aspects of each proposal. She must be able to effectively convey that information—using language, descriptions and explanations parties understand—thereby enabling parties to act based on their enhanced understanding.

> *Example.* A mediator should not say: "I don't know how else to explain to you the school district's discussion of the financial ramifications of your proposal to keep the neighborhood school open on weekends so that your children can use its facilities." She must find an effective way to explain such matters as liability and property insurance coverage, custodial costs, and pertinent contractual obligations with the affected unions. Otherwise, she assumes the risk of not getting an agreement simply because one party does not understand the constraints under which the other is operating.

A mediator also teaches and models negotiating behavior. Sometimes parties assume that negotiating requires certain types of conduct, such as shouting, lying or belittling an individual, or simply demanding a proposed solution without providing an explanation. A mediator, as a coach, educates participants—both parties and their representatives—about constructive negotiating behavior.

Resource Expander

A mediator must increase the range of resources that parties use to resolve their dispute. She can do this by generating additional information germane to the controversy, suggesting new ideas for settlement when the parties are stuck, setting up meetings between the parties and individuals to whom they had previously lacked access, and leveraging other services that can help the parties resolve their concerns.

> *Example.* A mediator might help a parent and her teenage child resolve some of their problems by identifying appropriate counseling services or planned recreational programs.

Agent of Reality

The mediator must be able to identify for each party what is doable in light of the interests and resources of the other parties to the discussion. If a party's proposal appears impractical or inflated, the mediator must help test its viability and ultimately emphasize that in light of the discussion the proposal appears unobtainable.

> *Example.* The parent group of the neighborhood elementary school is concerned about extremely low scores their children received on a standardized reading test. They blame the school principal for this dismal state of affairs and demand to meet with the school superintendent to insist that the principal be fired as an indication of the superintendent's commitment to correcting the situation. The superintendent adamantly refuses to meet under such conditions, but does offer to meet with the parents and the principal to discuss the school's reading program; the parents reject this suggestion and refuse to meet. A mediator, after canvassing the situation, should indicate strongly to the parents that their demand to have the principal fired simply will not be met—at least not at this juncture. If they want to talk to the superintendent or other school officials about improving their children's reading skills, they must first drop this demand as a condition for meeting, if not drop it altogether. The mediator does this not because she believes the superintendent is correct and the parents are wrong; she does it on the basis of her assessment that the superintendent will not change her position and that the parents must modify their demands if they want to have any discussions at all to address their concerns about test scores.

The mediator should not diminish the credibility of the process by exploring proposals that are impossible or outrageous. Parties want an accurate reading of each other—what they want and what they are willing to live with.

However, the mediator cannot be so gullible as to believe that she should make the parties consider *every* suggestion or offer that is made. The mediator serves the parties well by eliminating fruitless discussions that will never advance a negotiated agreement.

Guardian of Durable Solutions

The mediator should not impose on the parties her own judgment or preference as to how a problem should be resolved. But the mediator must consider the consequences of what people are agreeing to and try to ensure that the agreement they develop will last.

> *Examples.* Out of impatience to conclude the discussion, parties sometimes agree to do things that are not practical. Neighbors, for example, might agree to stop the periodic fighting between their nine-year-old children by forbidding them ever to play with each other again; but if the children are classmates in school, the agreement will not be honored. A tenant might agree to move out of his apartment in one week; but if there are no vacant and affordable apartments in the area, that won't happen. While remaining neutral, the mediator must try to prevent the parties from agreeing to solutions that will not work in practice.

Scapegoat

The mediator can be the lightning rod for the parties' frustrations and concerns. She sometimes serves as the blamepost on which parties hang their excuses.

> *Examples.* Parties want to express their frustration and anger at the obstructiveness and obstinacy of their adversaries. If they directly accuse each other of such behavior, however, they increase their mutual antagonism and jeopardize any potential agreement. What do the parties do instead? They loudly blame the mediator for being ineffectual. This enables them to communicate their frustration and growing impatience to each other without risking an immediate breakdown in discussions.
>
> Similarly, negotiators can tell their constituents: "We don't like the settlement, but the mediator claims this is all any of us can possibly obtain in these talks, and she refuses to schedule any more discussions,

so it was this or nothing." This face-saving device of blaming the mediator for the settlement terms serves several purposes: it enables the negotiators to continue to advocate their group's demands while modifying the group's position in order to reach an agreement. It also allows them to accept terms of settlement without having to acknowledge publicly that they have acceded to the other's demands.

Protector of the Process

The mediator is responsible for protecting the integrity of the mediation process as a useful vehicle to help parties resolve disputes. Sometimes a party has no genuine interest in talking with others about what she is doing or planning to do, but is merely using the mediator and the process as a tactical decoy to help achieve an end. The mediator must promptly quash any such effort.

> *Example.* A commercial developer agrees to participate in mediated discussions with a group of citizens who are concerned about plans to build a fish hatchery in their small seaside resort town. By agreeing to meet, the developer generates the expectation within the citizen's group that its concerns about plant size, environmental impact, and increased traffic over local roads will be openly discussed and resolved collaboratively. If the developer then refuses to provide requested information, periodically misses scheduled meetings, requests postponements because of "unexpected emergencies" and refuses to consider the strengths or weaknesses of any proposals but her own while simultaneously proceeding quietly to obtain the necessary authorization and permits to build the plant exactly as she wishes, then she is using the legitimacy of the process and the aura of "good-faith mediated discussions" to dupe her adversaries. The mediator cannot allow any party to subvert the process in this way.

These responsibilities—chairperson, communicator, educator, resource expander, agent of reality, guardian of durable solutions, scapegoat, and protector of the process—constitute the mediator's job. They make a mediator's presence a valued one, although they certainly are not designed to help win a popularity contest. That is as it should be; the parties must live with the agreement, not with the mediator. The mediator is a catalyst. Her presence makes a difference. A mediator's participation affects the dynamics of how disputants interact with one another. She cannot be careless in executing her tasks; an inept performance can antagonize parties, increase tension, and shatter the possibility for agreement. In other words, a mediator can do harm. It is nonsense to assert that since only the parties can accept terms of settlement, it does not matter whether the mediator performs her tasks well or haphazardly; she must perform the job conscientiously and constructively to help parties reach acceptable terms of settlement.

We now examine those personal characteristics and abilities that enable people to execute these functions capably.

Job Qualifications of a Mediator

What kind of person is a mediator? Is she a gentle peacekeeper? Is she a demanding, aggressive, high achiever? Should we picture Jimmy Carter, Jesse Jackson, or Mother Teresa?

To determine the personal qualities an effective mediator needs, adopt the perspective of a party to a dispute and answer this question: If a mediator were to assist in your dispute, what characteristics and skills would you want her to possess? Your list would probably look something like this:

1. *Neutral.* A mediator must have no preference that the dispute be resolved in one way rather than another. She helps parties identify solutions that they find acceptable without ganging up on anyone. Every disputant would prefer to have a mediator who always supports her viewpoint. But since a mediator cannot do that for everyone, each party wants someone who at least is not working against her. If a mediator is not neutral, then there is no reason for the disputants to trust her.

2. *Impartial.* A mediator must treat all parties comparably, both procedurally and substantively. Justice requires it and effectiveness demands it. She cannot address some persons informally but others by title, convene meetings at sites that are inconvenient to some but advantageous to others, ignore the special needs of parties with disabilities, or persistently encourage parties to consider settlement terms that benefit one side only.

3. *Objective.* A mediator must be able to transcend the rhetoric and emotion of the parties. She must analyze proposed solutions with detachment to assess their strengths and weaknesses accurately, thereby assisting the parties to achieve a more objective view.

4. *Intelligent.* Parties are looking to the mediator for assistance. Although parties must educate the mediator about the specific problem, they do not want to be handicapped by a mediator's slowness of mind.

5. *Flexible.* A mediator must promote, not retard, the fluidity of the discussions. If a party makes a casual remark indicating a change of position on

an issue but the mediator refuses to discuss it until the current agenda item is resolved, the mediator's rigidity becomes the source of the impasse. The mediator must manage the process and chair the discussions, but she must not do so in a lockstep manner, constricted by self-imposed blinders.

6. *Articulate.* A mediator must be verbally astute to communicate the thoughts, perspectives, and proposals of one party to another. A mediator must choose her words wisely. People grow weary of listening to mediators who cannot state matters clearly and intelligibly.

7. *Forceful and Persuasive.* A mediator must be forceful enough to convince disputants to be reasonable and flexible. Parties do not want a mediator who merely accepts on faith the claims of the disputants and then exhorts them to find a way to resolve their difficulties.

8. *Empathetic.* A mediator must be able to appreciate the thoughts, fears, history, and perceptions that underlie each party's proposals. Parties do not need someone to tell them to love one another, but they do need to feel understood. They want help resolving their practical concerns in the real world of power, rights, obligations, and possibilities—not in some utopia. The mediator's capacity for empathy gives them confidence that the alternative solutions they are exploring with the mediator will not ignore their needs.

9. *Effective Listener.* A mediator must hear and comprehend the concerns of all parties. If a mediator is constantly talking or asking questions, the parties will not believe she is interested in understanding their problems as they see them. A mediator, above all, must appreciate the wisdom of the saying "It is no accident that people are made with two ears and one mouth."

10. *Imaginative.* If a mediator cannot generate fresh ideas and different perspectives, she adds little value to the discussion. One need not be a genius to be imaginative. One way to resolve a dispute between siblings who are fighting over which television show to watch at 8:00 p.m. is to suggest that they record one show while they watch the other. Kids (and grown-ups, too) can get so wrapped up in arguing over trivial matters (who watched her program first last week, or who turned the TV on) that they overlook obvious solutions.

11. *Respected.* A mediator does not need to be famous, but she must be a capable individual whose presence, at the very least, does not constitute an insult to the parties. Everyone believes her own problems are important, and they are. Disputants want a mediator whose background or reputation lends stature to their discussions. Disputants feel confident that their concerns are being accorded respect if the chairperson of the town's biggest employer serves as mediator; conversely, suggesting that the mediator be "any citizen volunteer whether trained in mediation or not," might be both demeaning and useless.

12. *Skeptical.* The mediator must be comfortable operating in an environment where she entertains all information provided but remains healthily skeptical of its accuracy. Conflicting accounts are the norm in mediation.

13. *Able to gain access to resources.* A mediator must have sufficient energy and stature to gain access to those resources that are necessary or helpful for resolving the dispute. The parties might need to convey their concerns to the company president, mayor, governor, school superintendent, or some other official with significant power to influence the outcome. If the parties themselves do not have access to such resources, the mediator must fill the gap.

14. *Honest.* The mediator's integrity must be beyond reproach. Since the parties do not always trust each other, they must be able to trust the mediator. No one will trust someone who misleads or deceives.

15. *Reliable.* If the mediator says she will do something—gather certain information, contact particular individuals, or prepare a draft of the agreement—she must do it. Parties do not need a mediator who promises but does not deliver.

16. *Non-defensive.* A mediator must be able to absorb a party's venting frustration and criticism of the process or of the mediator. No apologies are required for best efforts, but the mediator must know when to take abuse and blame without comment and when to confront it.

17. *Sense of Humor.* A mediator must be able to smile and laugh, both with others and at herself. The deft use of humor can relax tensions, put people at ease, or make a point in a subtle way. No mediator should make an individual party the object of ridicule or the butt of one-liners, nor should humorous remarks be at the expense of particular groups or classes of people. But the mediator should not make the mistake of believing that serious business cannot be conducted with some laughter.

18. *Patient.* Every mediator knows that the shortest route to a settlement is not a straight one. A mediator must be prepared to manage the discussion through all the side streets that lead eventually to that destination. Parties want someone who will assist them no matter how long it takes. They do not want a mediator to tell them that their matter must be resolved in twenty minutes because she has to leave for a business meeting or tennis date. They do not want a mediator who acts like a stereotypical bureaucrat who simply processes their dispute along with hundreds of others. They want to be heard. They want to express their concerns in their own language. They want to tell the mediator what they believe is relevant to their dispute, rather than being restricted to responding to questions on a form. All this takes time, and while no one's patience is inexhaustible, the mediator should be the last person to lose it. The

mediator operates knowing that it often takes the first 90 percent of the total discussion time to resolve 10 percent of the issues and the final 10 percent of the time to solve the remaining 90 percent. The lesson is clear: the mediator cannot force a settlement; she must be prepared to take the time to listen to concerns and move the disputants toward agreement at a measured pace.

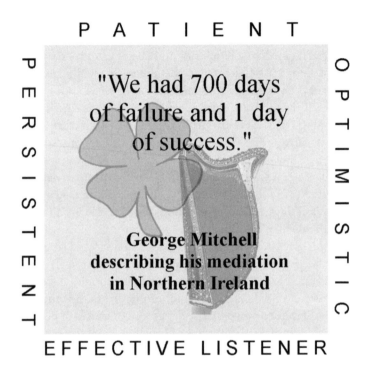

P A T I E N T

P E R S I S T E N T

O P T I M I S T I C

"We had 700 days of failure and 1 day of success."

George Mitchell describing his mediation in Northern Ireland

EFFECTIVE LISTENER

19. *Persevering.* The mediator must be able to persevere. Not naively, of course—not if there is no sign of progress. But every discussion, whether it lasts three minutes or three months, proceeds by spits and spurts, starts and stutters. Disputants become exasperated when it seems that they take three steps backward for every two steps forward. Even when agreement appears within their grasp, something can happen to set back the prospect for resolution. The mediator cannot quit. She must get past the exasperation born of fatigue and continue to press the parties to clarify details or reexamine the strengths and weaknesses of proposals. She must be prepared to go the distance without really knowing how far that is.

20. *Optimistic*. A mediator must be upbeat. She must charge the discussions with an electricity that gives people confidence that they can resolve their concerns. She must inspire them to believe in their ability to shape their own future. Consider a mountain climber who must cross a crevasse in order to survive. Is it possible? The objective facts are not encouraging: a greater-than-normal distance, heavy boots, inclement weather. But these "facts" ignore the climber's will to believe the feat can be done. Surely, the success of the leap will be affected by a belief that success is likely. A mediator must provide this positive element to the dispute settlement discussions.

But a mediator does not serve the parties well if she is a naive optimist or a pollyanna. She must be realistic and candid with all parties about the likelihood of success. Still, the mediator should not confuse being realistic with being an automatic nay-sayer. Nothing is more discouraging to disputants than always to be told why something *cannot* be done. Most people dislike the idea of being involved in a dispute; they want it resolved, and they do not need someone to reinforce their misery by reminding them of the hopelessness of their situation.

These are the characteristics and abilities that parties to a dispute want to see in their mediator. Obviously, none of us has all of these qualities in abundance all the time. But we do possess them in sufficient, though varying, degrees to enable us to execute the mediator's role effectively.

Now we know what the mediator's job involves and the qualifications required to perform it. So, humbled but excited by the challenge, we proceed. How do we get started?

5

Assessing Entry

Let us never negotiate out of fear; but let us never fear to negotiate.
John F. Kennedy

A mediator operates in a rich milieu, not a vacuum. He joins conflicts in progress that have a history and distinctive participants. The mediator must not begin by stepping on mines. He must scout the terrain. He must identify the players. He, together with the parties, must determine if mediation is appropriate. He must decide whether his presence would be constructive, and, if so, develop a plan for how to proceed.

PRIOR-TO Mediating: Anatomy of a Conflict

Although every dispute differs in its details, all disputes have a similar structural framework. We can ask the same questions and analyze the same components for every dispute. In some cases, the mediator will have the luxury of many days or weeks to analyze a dispute and scope out whether or how to proceed. In other situations, the mediator will have only a few moments after being handed a case by a school administrator, a court clerk or the director of a community mediation center. Whatever amount of time there is, the mediator must examine the following seven components: parties (P); resources (R); issues (I); options regarding process (O); rules affecting behavior (R); time constraints for resolution (T); and outcomes (O)-PRIOR-TO, for short. The mediator's first task is to apply this framework to the particular situation at hand. He must answer the question: What has happened PRIOR-TO his appearing on the scene? This information, in turn, will affect his plan for addressing the situation.

Gathering the information to answer this question, however, requires a clear understanding of the elements that make up these essential components of a dispute.

PRIOR-TO Entry: Examining the Components of a Dispute

Parties	Persons known to each other who advocate distinct, clashing positions on a given matter and have the apparent power to frustrate each other's actions or satisfy each other's concerns
Resources	People, programs, information, finances, and publicity to which parties and mediator have recourse
Issues	Matters, practices, or actions that in some way adversely affect some party's interests, goals, or needs
Options for process	Dispute resolution processes (in addition to mediation) that are available to the parties
Rules of behavior	Laws, institutional rules, professional codes of conduct, industry practices, and social conventions that establish the range of possible settlement options
Time frame	Deadlines within which outcomes must be developed
Outcomes	Possible dispositions of issues, varying in form, type and specificity

Parties (and Other Participants)

A mediator must distinguish between those persons who are merely *involved* in the dispute and those who are critical to its resolution. Every dispute involves people who are identifiable to and by one another. Disputants can have various types of relationships to one another; they can participate in mediated discussions as individuals, groups, corporations, or governments. A *party* is someone who is involved in a matter and whose agreement is necessary to resolve a particular issue or set of issues.

Identifying which people are both *involved* in the dispute and must be *parties* to its resolution is often easy. Two neighbors have no difficulty identifying their two ten-year-old sons as the only persons involved in a dispute over who will be pitcher first and who will be at bat. Similarly, for disputes among divorcing couples, landlords and tenants, supervisors and subordinates, homeowners and contractors, and professors and students, the parties to the dispute are easily identifiable. But some disputes are more complex, and distinguishing the parties to the dispute from the people involved in it can be considerably more difficult.

Suppose a homeowner wants to operate a day care facility out of his home. He applies to a government agency for approval. Some neighborhood residents want to prevent this development from occurring, other neighbors actively support it, and some do not care. Are all these persons involved in this dispute—if so, in what ways?

The dispute here appears to be between the homeowner who wants to operate the facility and those neighbors who oppose it. They would be *parties* to the mediated discussions since they have distinct, clashing positions on the matter, with the apparent power to frustrate each other's interests or satisfy each other's concerns.

What about the government official and the other neighbors? They are *involved* in the dispute, but should they be *parties* to the mediated discussions? If the government official operates under a policy mandate to establish as many residential day care facilities as possible, then he has a distinct interest in how this dispute is resolved; he is a party to the dispute and would assume a separate spot at the discussion table. But if the policy is simply to grant approval to all such proposals as long as they comply with statutory guidelines, then, although he is involved in the dispute in the sense that operating the facility requires his official authorization, he is indifferent to whether the neighbors agree to let it operate or not; he is not a *party* to the dispute.

The other neighbors can also be said to be *involved* in the dispute in the sense that they will be affected by the outcome. If the facility is approved, for example, they might have to drive more carefully at certain times of day. Indeed, one might claim that the entire community is involved, for in a limited sense all the following people are affected by the decision: the parents of the children who would use the facility; the local employers who experience increased absenteeism or low productivity when their employees must struggle to find adequate day care facilities for their young children; the children who would attend the facility; the workers who would be employed at it; the businesses that would prosper by virtue of increased purchases of supplies by this project; and all the taxpayers who might pay less in the future for special school programs, social services, or law enforcement activities if high-quality care were made available to people at an early age.

Should all these individuals be parties to the discussions? To answer this requires application of the same fundamental principles of individual and political morality that influence all our choices of a dispute resolution process. If we believe that decisions involving the location of day care centers should be made by anyone who is affected in any way, then the mechanism used must be one, such as voting, that enables everyone to express his preference. If, however, we prefer to have the matter resolved by those who perceive their interests to be most significantly affected by the proposed action, then the number of *parties* to the discussions is dramatically smaller than the number of persons affected by the ultimate decision.

In controversies like this one, we encourage those who are most tangibly affected by the matter to work out a satisfactory solution among themselves. There is no ready formula to answer the question: Who should be involved in the discussions? In the matter just described, two parties to the dispute seem obvious—the proponent of the facility and the neighbors who oppose it. But what if a citywide organization of "Parents for Day Care Facilities" took an active interest in supporting this application? Should its role be that of "concerned bystander," of a "constituent" who is "represented" by the person trying to establish the facility, or of a group with a distinct interest in the outcome that merits its taking a principal role in the discussions?

The challenge is clear: the mediator must identify the *parties*. Beyond the parties, other participants may be crucial for success: attorneys and other representatives, interpreters, witnesses, experts, and support persons. A mediator does not want to overload the process with unnecessary baggage, nor shortchange the resources from which solutions can emerge. Decisions about participants must be guided by the goal of helping the parties understand the matter better and develop interest-enhancing outcomes.

Resources

Each party to a dispute possesses certain resources: people, information, money, and access to others such as politicians or the news media. A mediator likewise has resources: time, experience, reputation, access to others, and support services. Levels of available resources have a dramatic effect both on the way discussions take place and on their outcome. Power relationships among the participants, for instance, vary according to their available resources and affect the range of probable settlement options; similarly, a mediator who is systematically deprived of essential information by the parties will be ineffective in developing leverage points for moving the parties toward agreement.

Before stepping into a dispute, a mediator must canvas the resources likely to be available.

Issues

Issues are those matters, practices, or actions that in some way adversely affect some party's interests, goals, or needs. Resolving a dispute means solving its issues.

Issues differ from facts, assumptions, principles, proposals and feelings. The mediator's role in helping parties identify issues clearly and thoroughly may be his most important contribution to the dispute settlement process. Think of how often a parent effectively stops a shouting match between his children simply by helping them to understand exactly what they are shouting about.

Sometimes the issues that a mediator uncovers PRIOR-TO further engagement are not the complete universe of issues. More issues arise once the mediation is underway. Nonetheless, getting a sense of what is at stake in a dispute—relationships, property boundaries, use of office space—will further an analysis of who the parties are and what resources might be available and helpful.

Options for Process

Practically speaking, the range of available process options for resolving a dispute depends on the people, resources, and issues involved. Four students who are arguing over who gets to use the school playground's handball court first will not sue each other to resolve the issue. But citizens protesting the construction of a high-voltage transmission line that will cross their property might initiate court action, seek protection from the legislature and the governor, and picket the offices of the utility company that proposes to construct the line.

Some people have a developed tradition or practice for resolving disputes. Some families have weekly family meetings where individual members can voice their complaints about events that have occurred during the week (such as household assignments). Unions and management bargain over such matters as wages and hours of employment; they know that their agreement will last for a specified time period and that they will have a chance to propose changes in the employment conditions when their contract expires.

Mediation may or may not be a desirable option for resolving a given dispute. People must assess its strengths and weaknesses and determine whether using it at a given time is constructive. That decision is made in light of the other available options, and a mediator and parties must understand the range of process options to decide whether mediation is a good choice.

Rules Governing Behavior

Some types of disputes are always resolved by applying particular rules. If an employee demands that his supervisor grant him an additional week's vacation, the dispute might be resolved by a straightforward application of the company policy governing vacation leave. If a student complains about a failing grade, the professor can simply point out the rules of the course with respect to grades.

In other contexts, it is not at all clear what law, rules, or principles apply, what they may require, and the extent to which they are binding. Disputes over affirmative action programs for hiring minority, female, and disabled individuals are plagued with ambiguities about what laws apply, what the principles of social justice require when trying to correct the ravages of discriminatory treatment, and whether certain actions are discretionary or obligatory.

A mediator and parties must appreciate that both the range of available dispute settlement processes and the possible outcomes are restricted by the degree to which issues in dispute are traditionally and systematically resolved by applying clear, agreed on rules or past practices.

Time Constraints for Resolution

Every dispute has a time frame; its sources vary. The nature of the issue may set the time frame. Some issues involved in cases of disruptive student behavior arise quickly and must be addressed rapidly if they are to be addressed at all. Other disputes require participants to spend more time resolving the matter because the issues develop more slowly, involve complex technical analysis, have numerous parties, or concern practices that none of the parties are in a hurry to resolve. Think of how long people have tried to negotiate a resolution of various problems involving Israel and its Arab neighbors.

Other factors can also affect the time frame of a dispute. The participants may create a time frame. If the union declares a strike deadline, then it has imposed a constraint on the ensuing discussions: settle by midnight or it will strike. Laws can set time frames. Business mergers are negotiated in light of the tax implications of specific proposals; if a newly adopted tax law will become effective as of a specified date, then that factor generates a tempo for the discussions. If persons are dealing with politicians whose political power might expire on Election Day, their talks proceed with an eye on the political clock.

If separated parents are negotiating over who will host their child's birthday party, the dispute must be resolved before the birthday. A mediator canvasses such possible constraints when deciding how best to proceed.

Outcomes

Dispute outcomes differ. Agreement is not always achieved even in cases where understanding is improved. When an agreement is reached, it may be written or oral. The parties themselves may implement the outcome, or they might leave the responsibility for doing so to others. The outcome may sever the parties' bond completely or tie them together on a long-term basis. Processes for monitoring compliance may exist either as a component of the outcome or independent of it. A mediator, PRIOR-TO entry, cannot and should not begin to guess the precise outcome of a dispute. Nonetheless, having a sense of the range of possible outcomes in disputes similar to the one being mediated helps the mediator envision relevant participants or technical needs; for example, in some court-based mediation programs, the agreement must fit on a Stipulation of Settlement Form and the terms of agreement must be those on which a judge could sign-off.

A mediator must learn what existed PRIOR-TO his entry so that he can decide whether or not to commit to trying to help resolve the situation. But how does the mediator go about learning what existed PRIOR-TO his arrival? There are some general guidelines that apply to a variety of dispute settings.

Some disputes are reported publicly. Racial tensions and fights among students at a high school are frequently publicized. To begin to get answers to what has happened PRIOR-TO his entry, the mediator can read the newspapers, watch the television accounts of the controversy, or search the internet for information. In other cases, he can talk with friends, acquaintances, or other sources that know people involved in the dispute or the parties to it.

He can read various historical documents, treatises, laws, and books to get the flavor of the dispute. If the dispute involves persons of particular ethnic, religious, or cultural backgrounds, the mediator can read about their traditions and mores. If the issues concern technical scientific matters, he must study them. If the disputants include representatives of a complex business organization, the mediator must become familiar with that corporation's range of activities and its organizational structure.

Some parties are sent to a mediator by an agency such as a court, counseling service, or community-based program following a screening interview. The mediator can review the data recorded by the person who conducted the initial interview to learn about the relationship of the parties, the nature of their dispute, or the results they seek. A mediator must size up a dispute before he commits himself to serving. Sometimes he can conduct his initial research efforts independently of the disputants themselves, but it is not always possible or appropriate to do so. Sometimes, the only way—as well as the best way—to get answers to what has happened PRIOR-TO his entry is by talking directly with the people involved in the dispute. If the mediator proceeds in that manner, however, he must always remember—and must inform the people to whom he talks—that the goal of such discussions is not to reach a settlement but to explore whether the parties should use mediation and whether the particular mediator should serve. In all such discussions PRIOR-TO deciding to serve as a mediator, the mediator must be mindful of maintaining neutrality and each party's perception of his neutrality, and conduct such discussions with promised confidentiality to all participants.

> *Example 1.* A female employee approaches her supervisor. She claims that one of her male coworkers has created a hostile work environment for her by continually making sexually offensive remarks to or about her. She demands that the offender be fired. The supervisor must acquire information regarding what has happened PRIOR-TO his involvement so that he will be in a position to evaluate the most appropriate way to handle the matter—whether by referring the issue to the human resources department for a formal investigation, by speaking individually with the alleged offender, by advising the employee to file charges with the appropriate government agency, by postponing all action for an identifiable time period, or by meeting confidentially with both employees in an attempt to mediate an agreement regarding their future conduct.

> *Example 2.* The board of deacons of a neighborhood church informs neighborhood organizations and youths that it will close the church's recreational facilities to use by neighborhood youths because of "continuing vandalism to the property." A group of forty parents and youths protest this decision by entering the church on Saturday afternoon and informing the board members that they will not leave until it reverses its decision. When the board chair refuses to convene a board meeting to reconsider its decision, the protesters escalate their proposal to a nonnegotiable demand. The protesters contact a local television reporter and tell the reporter of their plight, and his filmed report of the sit-in constitutes the lead story on the 6:00 p.m. local news broadcast. Parishioners promptly telephone board members.

Some support the board action and others protest it, but all express concern that the matter be resolved quickly so that religious services can proceed the next morning without incident. Various community organizations rally to support the protesters.

At 8:30 p.m. the board chair telephones a potential intervener he has never met who has a reputation as a concerned citizen and effective problem solver. The board chair asks whether he is aware of the situation at the church; he is not. The board chair asks for help in "solving" the situation. The man responds: "I don't know if I can. Let me talk with you and your board so that I have a better idea of what's happening and what you are prepared to do to resolve it. I'll stop by the church first to inform the people there that I'm going to meet with you and that I will want to have a similar conversation with them afterwards. I don't know if they will be willing to talk with me, but I can't do anything without first meeting with each of you. After talking with both groups, I'll have a much better idea if I can be of any help."

The mediator proceeds to conduct those conversations, learn what has happened PRIOR-TO his involvement, and then decide whether or not to COMMIT himself to serve.

Example 3. A couple decides that they want a divorce. They approach an individual and ask that he serve as a mediator in managing their discussions over financial matters and childrearing arrangements. In the first discussion, the mediator has them talk generally about their situation, their aspirations, and their expectations regarding the mediation process in order to assess whether the parties and the process are suitably matched.

The Decision to COMMIT

The mediator must learn what has happened PRIOR-TO his entry in order to make a critical decision: Will he COMMIT himself to serve as a mediator?

There are some obvious situations in which a mediator would decline to serve. If a husband and wife asked a mediator to help them resolve their controversy over the methods the husband uses to abuse his spouse or children physically, the mediator would decline to serve. Public policy condemns such behavior; our fundamental values prohibit letting people decide to beat up others or to get beaten up by others every Thursday night from 7:00 to 8:00 p.m., even if they insist that such arrangements are acceptable to them. Likewise, if members of a terrorist group disagree over which tactics to adopt in seizing a foreign airplane and request a mediator's assistance, most individuals (though, regrettably, not all) would refuse the request.

Other situations are not so clear-cut. The need to decide, however, is inescapable. On what basis does the mediator make that decision? He must integrate the information about what has happened PRIOR-TO entry with an assessment of the factors outlined below. His assessment will enable him to make an informed decision as to whether to COMMIT himself to serve.

The mediator analyzes each factor by answering its defining questions:

COMMIT: Factors Influencing a Mediator's Decision to Serve

C:	Commitment of parties to the mediation process exists.
O:	Organizational resources are available to the mediator and to all parties.
M:	Mediation is appropriate as a dispute resolution process for this situation.
M:	Matters in dispute are ripe for discussion and resolution.
I:	Incentives exist for all parties to settle their dispute through joint discussion.
T:	Talents of the individual mediator are suitable for serving in this particular situation.

Commitment (C)
1. Are the parties willing to talk with each other about the issues? Will they share appropriate information with the other side or the mediator?
2. Are the parties willing to decide matters jointly rather than simply talking with a view to getting the other side's input before making a unilateral decision?
3. Is each side willing to include all necessary parties to the discussion?
4. Are parties willing to use mediation as the primary dispute settlement process for resolving the agreed-on issues or, minimally, to use other procedures openly so that the simultaneous use of different forums will not secretly or suddenly sabotage the mediated discussions?

Organizational Resources (O)

5. Do the parties have the resources and capacity to participate meaningfully in the mediation process?
6. Does the mediator have the time to commit to participating in the discussions?
7. Does the mediator have, or have access to, sufficient clerical, administrative, and meeting facility resources?
8. Will the mediator have available from the parties, from independent third parties, or from personal resources adequate financial support to cover the actual costs of the service and, where appropriate, a fee for service?

Mediation's Appropriateness (M)

9. Is the power relationship among the parties balanced enough that one party cannot unilaterally dictate the outcome and force compliance with it?
10. Are the issues being submitted to mediation of sufficient breadth or importance to merit allocating mediation resources to help resolve them?
11. Are the applicable group or institutional rules sufficiently flexible in application or ambiguous in content to permit the parties to develop specific solutions acceptable to them?
12. Are all parties physically and emotionally ready to participate?

Matters in Dispute (M)

13. Do the parties believe that their interests and goals may be served by talking with each other?
14. Are the issues sufficiently tangible so that the parties can identify and resolve them by taking specific, agreed on actions?

Incentives to Settle the Dispute (I)

15. Are there incentives for the parties to settle the matters through mediated discussions?
16. Can the incentives for the parties to settle override personal, institutional, or hidden agenda items that might sabotage efforts to resolve the dispute?

Talents of the Mediator (T)

17. Does the mediator's personality mesh with those of the parties to the dispute so that he will be a constructive presence for their interaction?

18. Does the mediator's background, experience, and method of entry (invitation of the parties, with the approval of the governor, assignment by an agency, and so on) secure his initial credibility with the various parties?
19. Does the mediator possess the requisite knowledge regarding the negotiating process?
20. Does the mediator understand the matters in dispute (or is he willing to learn)?

Once a person has learned what happened PRIOR-TO entry, he can COMMIT to serve if he can answer "yes" to these twenty questions. It is then no longer a question of whether to mediate, but only a matter of doing it well.

Why Would Disputants Use Mediation?

Parties will support mediation when they believe that a mediator's presence will be helpful. What advantages do advocates derive by agreeing to use mediation?

Some parties do not trust one another. Although a mediator does not vouch for the credibility of each party, advocates know that no mediator with any pride allows the process to be abused by persons who continuously misrepresent facts, positions, or commitments; no mediator lets himself become a dupe of any of the parties. Thus the parties can gain some confidence in the credibility of each other's stance simply by virtue of the mediator's COMMITting himself to serve.

Some parties fear that others will agree to negotiate but will then engage in delaying or obstructionist tactics designed to abort the discussions while gaining a unilateral advantage. In mediated negotiations, such fears are minimized. The mediator's task is to establish the tempo of discussions and steer parties toward making tangible commitments to address one another's concerns. The mediator does not convene the parties simply so that they can meet and confer; his exclusive interest is not to establish a cordial atmosphere or good diplomatic relations, however important those things might be in a particular context. A mediator tries to propel parties into taking responsive and concrete action. If one or more parties are obstinate or engage in stalling tactics, discussions are not constructive and the mediator will end them.

A mediator can ask important, searching questions without inviting the hostile or defensive response that might erupt if the parties asked such questions of each other directly. A mediator, for instance, wants to make sure that everyone who should be involved in the discussions is present; he will pursue that matter carefully but thoroughly with the identifiable parties. But if no mediator were present and one party told the others that it would not proceed with discussions until certain parties or personnel were present, it would risk alienating them—and escalating both hostile rhetoric and actions.

No one likes to be responsible for breaking off discussions, for he may be accused of quitting because he is not getting everything he wants; it also increases the price that party will have to pay to resume discussions. But if a neutral participant, the mediator, indicates that he will not schedule further meetings because he believes there is little prospect for resolution at that time, then all parties avoid blame for the collapse of the talks and can renew discussions later on without first having to assign blame for the previous failure.

The decision to use a mediator has an important symbolic dimension. It represents a tangible expression of one's commitment to resolving issues through discussion. It underscores one's obligation to treat other parties to the dispute with equal respect and concern. It reaffirms one's willingness to take responsibility for making decisions, to be accountable to others for one's actions, and to remain open to considering others' points of view.

The value of such symbolism should not be underrated. Disputes often erupt quickly, parties engage in rhetorical flourishes, and positions immediately become hardened. Finding a face-saving way out of that situation is often difficult. Using mediation is not an acknowledgment of failure. Rather, using mediation reflects a sensitivity to the risks of continued hostility and to the costs of communicating by accident; it represents an informed judgment that engaging in discussion with the assistance of a trained neutral might be an effective way to regain control of one's fate.

Of course, parties can pay only lip service to participating in mediated discussions in good faith, while trying to subvert the process in other ways. That simply underscores how important it is for a mediator to make certain a person's actions match his rhetoric. But if a party wants to send a signal to the others of willingness to explore a resolution acceptable to all, one way of doing so is by calling for, or agreeing to use, mediation.

The overriding benefit that all parties derive from using mediation is that it forces an increased clarity in their communications. A mediator ensures that parties are articulate about their concerns and listen to one other. A mediator encourages the parties to make concrete proposals, identify priorities, and consider trade-offs. He structures the discussions so that parties can explore possible solutions without the intense pressure of having to make quick, non-retractable responses to one another. He helps enlarge the shared base of information on which the parties operate. He serves as a sounding board for a new proposal or idea that one party wants to advance. He alerts parties to occasions where they are over-estimating their strength or miscalculating that of their counterparts.

In short, if there is a chance that parties can reach better understanding and agreement, that chance should be optimized by using a mediator. If there is no perceived chance for resolution, using mediation can at least help the parties know clearly and precisely what constitutes their disagreement.

BADGER

The equation is now complete. Parties have agreed to use mediation; the mediator has learned what has happened PRIOR-TO his entry and has COM-MITted himself to serve. Mediated discussions now proceed.

The mediation session consists of six distinct components: (1) begin the discussions (**B**), (2) accumulate information (**A**), (3) develop the agenda and discussion strategies (**D**), (4) generate movement (**G**), (5) elect to have separate sessions (**E**), and (6) reach closure (**R**)—or BADGER. These six components are generally consecutive, though conversation is more fluid and dynamic than a linear construct portrays.

The badger is a small animal that persistently, patiently, optimistically and tirelessly pursues its goal. Put bluntly, the mediator will BADGER the parties towards a different understanding of one another, an enriched range of options, and an agreement that is responsive to each party's interests.

BADGER: The Components of the Mediator's Role

B	Begin the Discussions.
A	Accumulate Information.
D	Develop the Discussion Strategy.
G	Generate Movement.
E	Elect Separate Sessions.
R	Reach Closure.

Part 3

BADGER: Mediator Skills and Strategies

6

Begin the Discussions

We are what we repeatedly do. Excellence, then, is not an act, but a habit.
Aristotle

There are two aspects to beginning the discussions. The first involves taking care of the necessary procedural arrangements. The second deals with starting the actual meeting.

Set the Procedural Framework

Where will people meet? How many will be there? When will they meet? How long will the session last? Will there be food? Who will talk first? Who will sit where?

The mediator wants to ensure that meeting arrangements and procedures do not disrupt the discussions. She wants them handled well so that people feel comfortable as they start to talk with one another.

The mediator begins by taking care of these important details. Usually, after having consulted with the parties, she simply announces the framework and makes appropriate arrangements. Sometimes, however, these matters become issues of fierce debate among the parties and end up as the first topic for mediated discussion. In any event, no mediator thinks they are trivial. The procedural framework creates a space within which people must feel safe, and the mediator must construct it with care. Like any host, the mediator receives no compliments for handling arrangements well but will invite interminable haggling and destructive exchanges for botching them.

These are procedural matters that the mediator must regularly handle:

1. Date of the meeting
2. Time and length of the meeting
3. Place of the meeting
4. Number and identity of participants
5. Information exchange or material provided to the mediator ahead of time (in some cases)
6. Role of observers or interested groups
7. Room arrangement
8. Refreshments and meals
9. Rules of protocol (order of speaking, formality of discussions, record keeping, status of outcomes)

Although these seem straightforward enough, they can be devilishly complicated. If a mediator schedules a meeting for 11:00 a.m., does that mean the meeting will last only until lunch at noon? If only one party has to travel seventy miles to attend a meeting in the city where all of the other parties live and work, should the mediator change the meeting site so that everyone must travel thirty-five miles, or should she alternate meeting sites so as not to favor one group? If one group has only two negotiators, but the other has five negotiating team members and thirty "observers and supporters," should the mediator arrange a meeting site that accommodates eight or thirty-eight persons? The mediator must develop guidelines with a keen sensitivity to the impact that choices will have on the parties' interaction and the way in which the guidelines might affect her own image as neutral.

> *Example 1.* Two vice-presidents in a corporation are engaged in a continuing controversy over the type of computer system that will best serve the needs of their respective departments. Their boss schedules a meeting to analyze their concerns and resolve the matter. Because she schedules the meeting for a day that one of them had announced as a personal vacation day, one person immediately believes the boss favors her and the other feels at a disadvantage. That perception might generate costly future consequences in low morale and poor productivity, regardless of the outcome of the particular discussion.

> *Example 2.* A group of fifty concerned citizens are picketing in front of the city library on a Friday afternoon, demanding to talk with the director about proposed cutbacks in neighborhood branch library services. The director states she will meet with them on the following Monday if they stop their picketing immediately. The citizens tell a

news reporter who is covering the event that they have accepted the invitation to meet but have refused to call off their picketing because it is their constitutional right to engage in such activity. A journalist files a news story about the protest and the ambiguity surrounding the scheduled meeting. The library director contacts a mediator, states confidentially that she will go ahead with the meeting as long as the picketing does not result in violence, and asks for assistance in convening the meeting. The mediator talks with the director and the picketers, learns what has happened prior to her involvement, and makes a decision to commit to serve. The first topics she explores with each party relate to establishing who will attend the Monday meeting and structuring how the parties will deal with the media.

Chapter 5 highlighted the mediator's task of assessing—PRIOR TO the discussions—who should participate as a party in the process. That crucial task has an impact on all the procedural arrangements. While it is obvious that parties themselves should attend to enable them to understand one another better and develop mutually acceptable options, it is not unusual for attorneys or other representatives to argue that they are equipped to handle the matter without their clients. While it may be true that representatives can settle a dispute—given adequate authority—the absence of parties means that settlement is the *only* attainable goal. Conversely, some programs discourage attorney participation, fearing that attorneys will import an adversarial climate. While that may happen, it is also possible for attorneys to be thoughtful listeners, articulate spokespeople, and creative problem-solvers. Excluding them could represent a major loss for their own clients and for the other side who will be deprived of a more balanced understanding of the legal case. While witnesses and experts are not necessary to persuade a neutral decision-maker (since mediators do not decide the dispute), they can insert useful information that is sometimes more persuasive to each side than what an interested party would say. Experts can also offer novel solutions to problems. Additionally, parties sometimes need a support person in order to feel comfortable talking or making decisions. Where there are issues regarding language ability, neutral, professional interpreters are critical. In all cases, it is an understatement to say that the mix of participants will have a crucial impact on the session!

In addition to thoughtful crafting of the participant mix, a mediator must try to make the physical environment in which the discussions occur as conducive to constructive dialogue as possible. The mediator does not always have control over whether the sessions are held in a comfortable room with decent circulation, heat, or air conditioning. One can easily imagine, though, how much more difficult it becomes for the mediator to resolve a dispute if the parties are shivering in a cold room. Finding an adequate, though not necessarily luxurious, setting helps to put people in a more positive frame of mind. The mediator can almost always make sure the meeting room is clean and orderly before the parties enter. To the extent that the mediator can control such things as art work, lighting and furni-

> Sometimes when I consider what tremendous consequences come from little things . . . I am tempted to think . . . there are no little things.
> Bruce Barton

ture, aiming for both comfort and inspiration in the environment helps promote parties' capacity to persevere and to be creatively engaged.

The mediator should control where various persons are physically situated with respect to one another so that she helps advance communication, safety, party equality and mediator neutrality. Two principles guide her decisions:

1. Each distinct party to the discussion should have a separate, equal spot in the room. Their position should facilitate conversation among group members, as well as communication with other parties.
2. The mediator's position, insofar as possible, should be between the parties, equidistant from them, and closest to the exit door.

The first principle prohibits the mediator from arbitrarily clustering many different parties into only two "opposing" groups. She must not be constrained by the rectangular shape of most tables, which invites placement of parties opposite each other on each "side." Instead, she must arrange the furniture so that persons with distinct interests are equal, separately identifiable participants in the discussion process. No parent, having just separated four fighting children, would then line them up to talk with each other by automatically putting the boys on one side and the girls on the other. A mediator must not make a similar mistake.

This first principle also prevents a mediator from acting according to the erroneous belief that the most effective way to promote peace is to have members of different groups sit next to one another so that they will mingle. Doing this might be catastrophic. People have separate, and sometimes competing, interests. Those with similar interests must be able to render moral support to each other or consult among themselves before accepting proposed solutions. The existence of separate identities does not preclude a settlement. If a mediator tries to paper over these differences by having everyone "mingle together," she undercuts the very dynamic that will help them reconcile their interests. No business executive systematically ignores the fact that various departments within the organization have conflicting or competing interests, nor does she believe that the way to reconcile them is to mix up everyone's work stations so that no one thinks of herself as being a part of a department or section rather than "the organization."

The second principle is important in two ways. First, putting the mediator between the parties and in the middle reinforces the perception that she is neutral. If the mediator is sitting next to party A on one side of the rectangular table and party B is sitting alone across from them, then party B will quickly conclude that the mediator favors party A. The mediator must place herself equi-distant from the parties and close enough so that everyone can speak comfortably and be heard. Second, by sitting closest to the door, the mediator can unobtrusively prevent a party's frustration, anger, or impatience from derailing a session. When a party becomes annoyed, she may throw up her hands in disgust, shout obscenities, and move toward the door to leave. If the mediator is sitting closest to the door, she can get up quickly and, while moving backward toward the door but still facing all parties, say "I know you're frustrated. I'm not sure we'll resolve these matters here today. But I believe we've made some progress, and I'd like to give it one final shot. Please, let's sit down. If the matter is not resolved in another fifteen or twenty minutes, then all of us may decide to go home."

The angry party can then use the mediator as a scapegoat to return to her chair ("I don't think we'll accomplish a damn thing, but if you want me to stay for twenty minutes, I will.") and avoid any accusation that her behavior was boorish or uncalled for. The talks can continue because the mediator had physically placed herself so that she could quickly and without fanfare block the exit.

The goals of safety and communication suggest that the mediator may want to position the parties across from one another (with a table in between), so that there is a safety zone between the parties and it is easy to look and speak directly to the other side—or to turn and speak to the mediator. A triangular, round, or rectangular table would all support such an arrangement. Having no table would also support flexible communication, and the absence of a barrier between the parties might signal an expectation of trust, but the absence of a table may make people feel exposed, hence uncomfortable.

Having made these decisions, and assuming that the mediator succeeds in getting everyone into the same room at the same time, she must immediately set a positive, confident tone.

Get Started

The mediator is there to assist all parties to talk about their concerns, come to a better understanding of one another, and work toward an agreement. But she doesn't want them to start to do that too quickly. Her contribution involves helping the parties discuss those matters in a way that differs from the way they have done so in the past. The mediator will not help by having them replay the same anger and shouting that have been part of their previous, unsuccessful efforts to resolve the issues. She must first help them reorient the way they look at their situation.

The mediator wants to establish an appropriate tone for the discussion. She wants people to feel comfortable so that they can deal constructively with their concerns. She wants to establish appropriate expectations about what can and cannot be done, torpedo the gamesmanship that comes when one party tries to gain an advantage by talking first, and get the parties to have confidence in her ability to assist them. To achieve these objectives, the mediator should begin the session by making constructive opening remarks.

In formal settings, the mediator introduces herself, disclaims any bias in the matters to be discussed, explains the mediation process, and identifies the ground rules that will govern the discussion. In surroundings where everyone knows one another, the person in charge can modify these opening remarks accordingly. However the mediator starts, she must make certain the participants understand the goal of the process, everyone's role in it, and how the discussion will proceed. A teacher does not need to introduce herself to her students, a parent to her children, or a boss to her subordinates; but if a teacher or parent or boss wants to serve as a neutral intervenor, she must promptly clarify everyone's role and the discussion guidelines that apply. Here are some examples of introductory remarks:

Informal.

A dispute between two high school students involved in a food fight in a high school cafeteria is stopped by their mathematics teacher, who is on lunchroom duty:

> Jorge, Alex—What's going on? This isn't like you. The two of you could be in a lot of trouble for doing that. Unless you work it out right here and now, I'll have no choice but to send you to the principal.
>
> I don't know what happened, so tell me one at a time. Jorge, you start. Alex, don't interrupt; you'll have your chance when Jorge's finished. No cursing. No name-calling. Just listen to each other. Both of you have to be in class in ten minutes—you've got to work this out before then. Jorge, begin.

Formal.

A dispute between two neighbors is referred to a Neighborhood Justice Center.

> Good morning. My name is Wilson Follett, and I have been assigned by the Barrington Neighborhood Mediation Center to assist you today. I have not met either of you before, nor do I know anything about the matters that have brought you here.
>
> Before we proceed, I want to be sure that I have spelled everyone's name accurately and that I am pronouncing it correctly. Could each of you please introduce yourself? Thank you.
>
> I would like to take a couple of minutes to describe for you what my role will be in our discussion this morning and the goals and guidelines for our conversation. My job is to listen as carefully as I can to what each of you have to say regarding the concerns that have brought you here so that I, as well as each of you, have as rich an understanding of the situation as is possible. Based on that understanding, we will then

work as hard as we possibly can to explore ways to address your concerns that are acceptable to each of you. I have no authority to tell you what you must do. My job is to help clarify your concerns and examine with you how they might be resolved. If we can identify ways to solve these matters that both of you accept, then I will write your agreement, if you request me to do that, have each of you sign it, and then I will sign it as a witness. Both of you will be given a copy of the agreement.

Let me suggest how we will proceed. I will ask you, Mr. Rodriguez, as the person who first brought this matter to the attention of the Center, to speak first. When Mr. Rodriguez is finished speaking, Mr. Tomelli, you will have an equal opportunity to explain your concerns. As listening is so critical, while one person is talking, I ask that the other not interrupt him. Can you both agree to that guideline? I have given each of you some paper and a pen; if something is said that you want to respond to or to remember, simply jot a note to yourself so that you can talk about it when the other person has finished speaking.

This is a private conversation; whatever is said here remains in this room. I will be taking some notes so that I will not overlook or forget any concerns you raise; at the end of our discussion, however, I will destroy my notes, so that the only record of our conversation will be your written agreement if you make one. I am mentioning confidentiality to encourage you to speak freely here. There are exceptions to confidentiality—one concerning child abuse was explained by the staff when you arrived.

There may come a time during our discussions when I will want to speak with each of you separately. Meeting that way lets me discuss with you in greater detail some of the concerns and possible solutions that we will be talking about. I will let you know if and when I think such a meeting will be helpful.

I will stay as long as is necessary and as long as we are making progress to assist you in resolving these matters, and I presume that you share a similar commitment.

Since this room is very small and there are no windows, I ask that no one smoke while we are meeting. Please turn off your cell phones.

Are there any questions before we begin? If not, Mr. Rodriguez, please tell us about the matters that have brought us here today.

Beginning effectively is extremely important. If the mediator is hesitant, rambling, disorganized, or disrespectful, the parties will not have any confidence that she can help them. If the mediator presents herself as a person who is confident, articulate, and decisive, the parties instinctively will trust her. The adage that you "never get a second chance to make a first impression" should inspire every mediator to practice and perfect her opening remarks.

But beginning effectively is more difficult than it seems. The mediator can omit items, make choices that backfire, or use language that jeopardizes her neutrality.

The mediator does not want to forget to mention specific guidelines because it undercuts her credibility if she is perceived as someone who makes up the rules as she goes along. After all, if the mediator forgot to mention a rule about privacy or interrupting, what else might she have forgotten to mention?

The mediator above makes choices in his opening remarks. He introduces himself as "Wilson Follett", rather than "Dr. Follett". Should he address the parties by their first names, as "Mr.", "Mrs.", or "Ms.", by their titles, or by some combination of these? By introducing himself as "Wilson Follett" he has signaled that last names will be used, though he has left the possibility of first names open. He has stated what authority he does *not* have as well as what he can do. He has clarified expectations regarding smoking and cell phones. Some decisions might immediately alienate one of the parties (for instance, the one who wants to smoke); some decisions cannot be changed once they are made (the mediator cannot begin by asking the parties to address him by his first name, Wilson, and twenty minutes later demand to be addressed as Mr. Follett). The mediator knows that such choices must be made and plans accordingly.

Finally, the mediator must use language that is jargon-free, precise, and consistent with a stance of neutrality. Think of how easy it is to botch this:

JARGON:
- I'm here as a mediator. I am completely unbiased. My job is to assist you negotiators in overcoming your impasse. (*What is a mediator? What does it mean and is it possible to be "completely unbiased"? What is a negotiator? An impasse?*)

CUMBERSOME:
- What I am going to do here today is to explore with you in great detail exactly what it is that brought you here. I want to get your honest feel-

ings about these matters. I want you to speak freely, openly, and forthrightly—don't hold anything back—and tell me in your own words exactly what is on your mind and how you would like to see things resolved. If each of you identify ways to resolve these matters that are compatible with one another, then, of course, the dispute is resolved. But if you identify ways to resolve these matters that conflict with each other— and I would presume that would be the case since otherwise you would have settled this before coming here . . . (*C'mon, man, get to the point!*)

PREJUDICIAL:

- Mr. Tadiken, tell me your side of the story. (*What do you mean, my "side"? I'm going to tell you the truth. Do you think I'm a liar?*)
- Mrs. Austin, why don't we begin by your repeating the allegations that you made against Mr. Castro at the staff meeting. (*Allegations? Nonsense! Those are facts.*)
- Mrs. Lincoln, since you are the person who was harmed and are seeking a remedy, we will begin with you. (*How do you know she was harmed? Is this a kangaroo court?*)

We all say things we later regret. A mediator, however, does not have that luxury if she wants to be effective. She must shape her language to fit the role.

The mediator knows that she must take care in preparing for and starting the discussions. She should plan and practice accordingly.

Once a mediator has concluded her opening remarks, what happens next is spontaneous. The mediator has very little idea what she is about to hear or what options exist. She does not know where the discussion will lead. But that does not mean that she lacks the skills to be of assistance. She will listen carefully and question thoughtfully. She will always use language that reorients the way parties view their challenge. She will consciously deploy multiple options and strategies for directing the discussions.

The mediator is like an orchestra conductor who is directing a group of musicians who are improvising their music rather than playing a composed work. The conductor knows about various forms of music, different harmonic structures, and the sounds and range of the various instruments; her challenge, like that of the mediator, is to get all the players of the violins, trumpets, flutes, drums, and other instruments—the parties to the dispute—to develop their respective parts in such a way that together they create a viable piece of music with all orchestra members contributing, rather than a cacophony of harsh sounds.

7

Accumulate Information

If we could read the secret history of our enemies, we would find sorrow and suffering enough to dispel all hostility.

Henry Wadsworth Longfellow

The parties have lived with their conflict. They are familiar with its dynamics and tensions. They feel its pressure. The mediator must learn this history as rapidly as possible.

The mediator gathers information with a purpose. He wants to understand the dispute—how the parties experience the "story" they tell. He wants to know what concerns, both substantive and emotional, must be addressed for all parties to settle their dispute. The mediator will not learn everything there is to know about the people he is serving. His interaction with the parties is relatively brief; he will get a glimpse of only a small slice of their lives. So he focuses on discovering information that will further a constructive dialogue. He prompts parties to describe the situation as precisely as possible so that everyone—most importantly, the other side—has a full understanding of the challenge. He targets the concrete matters in which they are entangled—the issues. He elicits common interests. He extracts rules, principles, values, law and customs that are important to the parties. He strives to have the parties articulate their feelings and identify their options if the dispute does not settle.

To accumulate information effectively, mediators must do five things:

1. Listen carefully.
2. Record notes selectively.
3. Ask helpful questions.
4. Support communication in nonverbal and verbal ways.
5. Mine the conversation for "gold."

Listen Carefully

Listening effectively to what someone is saying consists of more than just hearing sounds. One listens to understand the message the speaker is trying to communicate. To listen well is to capture the entire message. Listening skills prevent one from short-circuiting or contaminating that message-sending process. Here are some guidelines that a mediator can follow to insure he receives all that is sent:

> *Concentrate.* Minimize distractions: wear comfortable attire; eat prior to mediating so hunger does not distract you; put extraneous papers and cell phones away. Take notes selectively so as not to interfere with the capacity to listen.

> *Maintain Focus.* People cannot talk as fast as others can listen. A mediator should not use the overlapping time to daydream or worry about something else. Good posture—with the mediator's body oriented towards the speaker and arms relaxed and open—is helpful.

> *Be patient.* One cannot hear, let alone be certain he has captured what someone else is saying, if that person is not given a chance to complete his statements. Sometimes parties repeat themselves. Some speakers are hard to understand. A patient listener allows a speaker the freedom to tell his story—even if the telling is less than perfect.

> *Don't interrupt.* One cannot listen while talking. It is tempting to interrupt a party by asking questions or providing information, but such behavior both disrupts a speaker's chain of thought and exhibits unhelpful conduct that other participants might copy.

> *Understand without judgment.* Often one stops listening because he does not like what is being said, who is saying it, or the way it is being said. He assumes he knows the argument, and, since he disagrees with it, stops listening. A mediator cannot argue mentally with the speaker. Understand first; evaluate later—much later.

Record Notes Selectively

While listening attentively, it is appropriate for a mediator to take notes. But they are for his purposes only. Any final document reflecting the agreement of the parties will be separate. That fact clarifies the purpose of a mediator's note taking: he records only information that will be useful in helping the parties understand one another better, structure the discussion, and capture proposals and agreement terms. If the mediator's memory is so keen that he can remember everything that was said—and by whom and when—then he has no need to take any notes at all.

What does a mediator record in his notes? He jots down the names of everyone in the room so that he can address people by name. He captures parties' common interests to provide aspirational goals for the negotiation. He records the issues in dispute that have been identified because he wants everyone to agree on what must be resolved. At times, he may record the precise wording of proposals so that there is no ambiguity. A mediator notes the order in which the parties present their settlement proposals so he can detect whether they are displaying flexibility and movement toward agreement or are escalating their demands. It is important for a mediator to note what has been discussed with only one party in a separate session so that he will not breach confidences. For all these purposes, note taking is useful.

Taking notes, however, is not the same as making a verbatim transcript of the proceedings. By its very nature, note taking is selective. A mediator does not, and should not, take down everything that is said. We often believe that by taking notes as someone talks, we will listen more attentively, demonstrate to the speaker our keen interest in what he is saying, and affirm the seriousness of the occasion by recording it in tangible form. Rubbish!

When a mediator writes things down, he disrupts eye contact with the speaker, thereby losing the ability to capture what is being communicated nonverbally. A mediator can become so preoccupied with his notes that his listening loses pace with the speaker's presentation. Eventually he falls behind and has to interrupt to ask questions that have already been answered. Since a mediator, at first, does not know where the presentation is leading, he has no idea which matters are relevant to the dispute and which are not. In his desire not to omit anything that might be important, he may record almost everything that is said, thereby converting his notes into the very transcript that he did not want to create.

Most dangerous of all, by taking too many notes, the mediator may become a captive of the parties. Suppose, for example, that during the course of a mediation involving two neighbors, one states that his neighbor's seventeen-year-old son, when his parents are not around, has loud parties where he and his friends smoke marijuana. If the mediator writes that down, what will the mother of the seventeen-year-old now believe about the mediator? She will be convinced, with some justification, that the mediator believes that her son has committed a criminal offense. What will the parent do to protect her son's reputation? She will deny the accuracy of the allegations and then retaliate by charging her neighbor with having engaged in illegal conduct, whether such a charge is true or false; the parent will then wait for the mediator to demonstrate his neutrality by recording her accusations as well. This is a prescription for the discussion to disintegrate rapidly into a shouting match.

A mediator wants note taking to assist, not undercut, his efforts to help the parties reach agreement. He must trust his memory and listen attentively. If he does not remember something that later becomes important, he can always ask the party to restate the point.

Ask Helpful Questions

Most people, once they say everything they need to say and feel heard, become more open to hearing others. Many people, if they talk long enough, say things that are inconsistent with their earlier remarks or suggest areas of possible accommodation. Those are levers the mediator can use to encourage shifts and settlements. Thus, the mediator's task is clear: keep people talking. Different forms of questions elicit different information and emotional responses. The mediator wants to develop a rich information base in a short period of time in a climate that invites conversation. What types of questions are most helpful to achieve that?

Start-Up Questions

How can a mediator get people talking, particularly if someone is reluctant, uncomfortable with language, hesitant, nervous or shy? He asks questions that invite the party to discuss specific events or situations with which the party is familiar. These are questions that should be easy for her to answer—in the sense that the party knows the information to share. Questions that include the terms *what, who, when,* and *where* are particularly effective start-up questions:

- Please begin by telling us *what* happened that led to your bringing this concern about your supervisor, Mr. Atkins, to mediation?
- *Why* don't you start by telling me *when* you became a tenant in Mr. Keating's building?
- Could you tell me *where* the incident we will discuss occurred?

These questions force the speaker to start sharing information, but they are not threatening or accusatory in tone. They should help open the door of discussion so that the mediator can quickly follow up with open-ended questions.

Open-Ended Questions

Open-ended questions let the party respond by elaborating on a subject in his own words. Questions that include *what*, as well as phrases such as *tell me more*, generate this response:

- Could you please explain *what* brings you here today?
- *What* happened next?
- Could you *elaborate* on that, please?

Open-ended questions elicit the most information in the shortest amount of time. The parties know best what has happened, or at least what they believe has happened. The mediator's task is to get them to describe it. Using open-ended questions accelerates that process.

One way people reveal their priorities is through their choice of words and topics and the emotions they use to express themselves. The mediator cannot learn whether someone is angry, upset, committed, or nonchalant if all the person does is answer "yes" or "no". Open-ended questions also serve the parties' interests in having the mediator treat them in a dignified, respectful manner, as questions in this form give people a chance to explain the dispute in a way that is most comfortable for them.

Open-Ended but Focused Questions

These questions invite persons to answer in their own words but they target the subject matter. After the parties' initial presentations, the mediator may use such questions to focus the parties' comments on things related to the issues in dispute. For instance, he may ask:

- Will you please tell me more about *the party that occurred last night*?
- Will you tell me *how you conducted the research for this project*?

In so doing, the mediator directs the party to focus his remarks on a specific subject rather than wandering aimlessly.

Justification Questions

These are *why* questions:

- Can you tell me *why* that wage proposal is unacceptable?
- Could you explain *why* you object to Marco's proposed division of project responsibilities?

There are two levels of response to such questions: substantive and perceptual. Both are important to a mediator.

The substantive response displays the person's rational justification for adopting or rejecting the proposed solution. "If X is the problem, then Y is one solution because it relates logically to X in the following way. . . . But we prefer solution Z to Y because it advances the welfare of our group significantly more than does solution Y, and the cost of solution Z to you is only slightly more than what you would incur under solution Y." The mediator presses to make certain the party's position is internally consistent and rationally persuasive. A credible response either solves the issues or highlights those concerns that the settlement terms must satisfactorily address.

The perceptual response forces the party to reveal whether the grounds for promoting or resisting a proposed solution relate to the personalities of the parties rather than the logic of the solution. Parties might find a solution plausible but resist it because of who suggested it ("If the finance department proposed it, there must be a catch someplace"); the need to take time to convince others ("I understand that you want to save money by buying new software and state-of-the-art robots. But that will result in twenty-seven persons in my unit losing their jobs with no prospect of being employed elsewhere in the company. I can't go along with this proposal until I've had some time to talk with my people and prepare them for this move—the last thing we need is a protest and a work slow-down"); or the fears, concerns, or dreams that the proposal does not address ("If we agree to settle this job discrimination complaint rather than contest it through the administrative hearing and court process, how will we guard against setting a precedent that gives us the reputation of settling any complaint, however frivolous it might be?"). If the mediator gets this type of response to the question of "Why?" or "Why not?," then he must adopt a strategy to meet it, for agreement at the substantive level is a necessary but not sufficient condition for settlement; parties must be *psychologically* ready to settle as well.

Leading Questions

A leading question has two components: first, the answer is contained in the statement of the question; second, the person who is asked the question can respond only by saying "yes" or "no." Here are some examples:

- You were late in submitting the report, weren't you?
- You left the babies unattended while you were playing tennis, didn't you?
- When you leased the apartment to Mr. Domrin, all the appliances were in working order, weren't they?

A person who asks a leading question accomplishes one of two goals: either he makes the person to whom the question is put defensive, flustered, and uneasy, or he makes sure that he, the questioner, tells the "facts" rather than allowing the person being questioned to do so.

One can readily understand why a lawyer conducting a cross-examination asks leading questions. The questions contain conclusions and are accusatory in tone. They are not designed to foster discussion. They do not generate new ideas. They are designed to establish the anchor points around which all consequences must pivot.

As a rule, a mediator should not pose leading questions. It is a mistake for a mediator to believe he can save time or focus discussion by asking leading questions. Parties to such a verbal onslaught become defensive, tense, and no longer consider the mediator neutral. Such a reaction impedes discussions rather than enriches them.

There are, however, some occasions when a mediator may want to ask leading questions. Such questions may be appropriate in a private meeting with a party—a caucus. How a mediator occasionally might use leading questions to generate movement toward settlement will be addressed in chapter 10 on caucusing.

A mediator always acts purposefully, and this includes asking questions. He must think not only about what information he is trying to get but also about how he formulates questions to get it. He does not ask many questions. Particularly in the early stages of gathering the facts, the mediator must get the parties to present the maximum amount of information with the least possible interference.

Support Conversation

There are both nonverbal and verbal ways for a mediator to encourage conversation and check his understanding of what has been said, although he must always be sensitive to when and where he does it.

Nonverbal Communication

Not all communication is verbal. By turning his chair and facing a speaker, the mediator reinforces his commitment to give the speaker undivided attention. By burying his head in his notes and gazing out the window while a party is talking, he communicates a lack of interest in what the speaker is saying.

Likewise, a mediator's physical appearance communicates a sense of respect or disrespect for the parties and their problems.

A mediator communicates the need for patience by not interrupting others. If he stands up while the parties are sitting and tells them not to interrupt each other again, he signals forcefully to the parties that their verbal exchanges have exceeded acceptable limits. He communicates a sense of urgency by glancing down at his watch before asking a question. If the mediator is the only person in the room who is not laughing at a joke that someone has told, people will wonder whether he is also communicating an inability to appreciate humor or empathize with other feelings such as sorrow, pain, or loneliness.

A mediator can also communicate nonverbally his assessment of the credibility of a party's description of events or the plausibility of a proposed solution. If a mediator frowns as he hears one party present proposed solutions, or if he throws his pen into the air and pushes his chair back from the table, he is communicating the judgment that the proposal is a disaster. On the other hand, if the mediator suddenly stops writing as one party presents his proposals, slowly and quietly places his pen on the paper while looking directly and pensively at the party who is speaking, then the mediator is signaling to the speaker and everyone else that what is being said is worthy of everyone's attention.

The lesson is clear: a mediator must be aware of this dimension of conduct. He must marshal his actions to convey the idea he wishes to communicate. He cannot control how parties interpret all of his nonverbal behavior any more than he can always be certain they have understood everything he has said. At the very least, however, he can make certain that his nonverbal actions are consistent with his verbal statements.

Just as the mediator communicates nonverbally, so do the parties to the dispute. People say things with anger or fear. They communicate a feeling of nervousness or impatience by tapping their foot or pen or speaking with a voice that shakes. They communicate a sense of panic or vulnerability with their eyes, a sense of pride or defiance with their posture. The mediator must be attuned to capturing messages from these communication sources.

Verbal Reinforcement and Clarification

A mediator actively seeks to ensure he understands the parties' communications and to demonstrate that understanding to them. In doing so, he displays a level of interest and respect that encourages disclosure and further communication.

A mediator can ask questions to clarify previous statements. He can attempt to summarize in his own words what was said. He can, in a separate session with the party, try to confirm his understanding of what the party said by identifying the emotion that the statement exhibits or the priority ranking the party attaches to particular items.

However, a mediator should never try to show his understanding of what was said by simply repeating back to the parties in their own words what they just said. For example, at the close of one party's presentation, a mediator should NOT respond as follows:

> Let me make sure that I understand what you are saying. You stated that the facilities at the neighborhood school, including the swimming pool, the gymnasium, and art rooms, are adequate and ideal for your children to use after school, on weekends, and during the summer. You said that the families in your neighborhood consist of hardworking, honest, religious people. You said that there are two real reasons why the school district refuses to open up its facilities for use to neighborhood residents during those non-school hours: first, the school board members are a bunch of snobs who don't understand how difficult it is to have kids engaged in healthy activities because they are rich enough to send their kids to summer camp or enroll them in private lessons; second, the teachers are too lazy and selfish to spend time supervising your children after the class day has ended. You said that the parents in the neighborhood would be willing and capable of supervising the children at their school during the non-school hours.
>
> Have I understood everything that you have said and proposed? Fine. Now, would the school district representative like to address himself to these proposals?

This mediator has made three serious mistakes. First, a mediator is not simply a tape recorder with a playback button; if he understands what was said, he should show it by summarizing the statements in his own words.

Second, from the moment a person begins to serve as mediator, he should try to reorient the way the parties view their situation. He starts to do this by always describing the dispute in less explosive, nonjudgmental language. Harsh language is an important barometer of parties' feelings, but restating insults rarely helps promote party dialogue and collaboration. For instance, a mediator must not regurgitate the parents' accusation that the school board members "are a bunch of rich, insensitive snobs"; rather, he might note that the parent group feels strongly about their children having recreational opportunities and facilities during nonschool hours and is asking that the school district make the facilities at the neighborhood school available to them. The mediator should not repeat the parent group's charges that the school district employs "lazy teachers"; instead, he should note that the parent group is offering to handle supervision of the children at the school by assigning that responsibility to various neighborhood residents.

Summarizing the parents' concerns in this way diffuses any personal attacks and helps to shift the parties' attention to the issues they must resolve and the proposals being made, rather than on attacking one another. In the process, the mediator provides the parties with a new, shared point of departure for considering settlement options. Those who assert pejoratively that a mediator is simply being "diplomatic" when he uses different words to characterize the elements of a dispute fail to appreciate the strategic leverage he obtains through the deft use of language.

Third, disputing parties have strong emotions. Despite what the mediator has said about his neutrality, if one party hears the mediator repeat allegations, assertions of fact, or conclusions in the language of his adversary, then he will conclude, fairly or not, that the mediator believes everything the other has said before he has even given everyone a chance to state what has happened or what should be done. If that occurs, the mediator's potential contribution may be irreversibly diminished. It does no good for him to turn to the party and say: "I'm not agreeing with what he is saying—I'm simply indicating that I understand what he has said." Parties hear such summaries differently, and the mediator is left in the position of "protesting too much."

The mediator might properly conclude that it is important to summarize his understanding of the parties' presentations to reassure them that he has grasped what is at stake or to establish his credibility by displaying mastery over the technical details of their proposal. But he must proceed with care.

Mine the Conversation for "Gold"

Listening carefully, recording only targeted notes, using helpful questioning formats and supporting parties' communication are critical performance skills, but a mediator must do more when accumulating information. He must know what he is listening for—what elements of the conversation will turn two monologues into a dialogue.

Imagine the following statement:

My brother is a selfish, rich, arrogant, sexist capitalist who cares only about money and shouldn't be able to call himself my brother. He is using his position as executor of our parents' estate to rob me and my child, Jason, of our heritage. He pretends to like Jason by inviting him to his home, but then claims that the financial support our deceased parents gave towards Jason's education was a "loan" that I must repay—

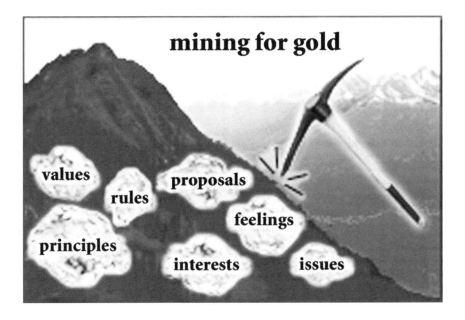

that would be $60,000 that he says he'll take out of my share of the estate. Over my dead body! So, he'll just get a bigger portion. I will take him to court before allowing that. I don't care how much it costs. It wasn't a loan! It was loving grandparents supporting a needy grandchild. Our parents always believed in supporting education. And he wants to sell our family farm to developers. How can he take this property and rape it? He has no respect for our parents' intention that the land would remain pristine and be protected. We should sell to the Nature Conservancy—not developers! Actually, I'd like to keep the farm for future generations. On top of every other insult, he took

Jason to a nightclub on Jason's birthday where there were strippers. What kind of values does that teach a kid? He should be helping him meet decent people rather than corrupting him.

Listening to this statement, most people hear insults, put-downs and threats. But a mediator hears it differently: he finds "gold nuggets" that are building blocks for constructive conversation. What should a mediator be listening for?

Interests

Interests are the silent, powerful movers behind positions that parties take. There will be no resolution if someone believes that his primary interests have not been respected, secured, or advanced. The mediator might conclude from the statement above the speaker has at least three that she wants met: Jason's development and well being; her brother's respecting the wishes of their parents; and their collectively maintaining family connections and traditions. It is possible that her brother shares some or all of these interests; if so, those constitute *common interests*.

Negotiating Issues

Negotiating issues are those distinct matters or behaviors that frustrated a party's interests and resulted in the need for mediation. The issues become the subjects around which an agreement is built—if the parties want an agreement. Issues constitute the bargaining agenda. The issues the speaker referenced above could be described as: the $60,000 paid for Jason's education; the family farm; and Jason's birthday celebration.

Proposals

Proposals are suggestions or offers for the resolution of issues. Like interests and issues, proposals can be hard to hear if they are embedded among threats and insults. The opening proposals in the example above are: the $60,000 payment should be treated as a gift from the grandparents to Jason; the farm should be retained by the family or sold to the Nature Conservancy; and social events sponsored by the speaker's brother should promote Jason's career and moral development.

Feelings

Feelings are frequently hurt in an atmosphere where interests are frustrated, insults are felt, and misunderstanding abounds. The speaker in the example above may feel angry, frustrated, upset, and unloved. Once those feelings are expressed— and understood—they can be addressed and often change.

Principles, Values and Rules

Most people are governed by values, principles and rules that guide conduct. Laws (and our understanding of them) also provide an important guidepost. The mediator listens carefully to learn the parties' central tenets. The principles each party holds dear will need to be reflected in the resolution. The speaker above believes that:

- Executors should not engage in self-dealing.
- Grandparents should support the education of needy family members.
- Family land should be protected and preserved.
- Nightclubs with strippers are not appropriate places to take young people.

As each bargaining issue is examined, these tenets—and ones raised by her brother—will be addressed.

These building blocks—and others noted in later chapters—are what mediators listen for. They enable a mediator both to organize the information that is shared—or hurled—by the parties and distinguish between those comments to which he will invite further discussion and those that will drop by the wayside. No other intervener or counselor listens to disputing parties in this distinctive way.

The mediator must remember that events affect different people differently. A mediator does not listen effectively if he always anticipates what someone will say, completes his thoughts for him, assumes that this person's problem is the same as ones he has dealt with before, or "expedites" the process by asking a series of questions. The mediator does not know what has happened. He wants people to state their concerns. As they do, they not only enrich his appreciation of the situation but also help the parties understand each other more clearly, perhaps for the first time. Then it is time to move ahead.

During this early stage of the discussion, the mediator's posture is to be as supportive and non-disruptive as he can. The mediator should keep quiet and let everyone talk, and talk, and talk, always knowing what he is listening for.

He must not act precipitously. His patience will always be tested, if for no other reason than the parties might believe that a mediator who is not talking or asking lots of questions is not "doing anything." But that perception will be effectively addressed shortly. Once a mediator is confident that the parties have shared the landscape of their dispute, he moves confidently to help them reshape its terrain.

8

Develop the Discussion Strategy

The greatest challenge to any thinker is stating the problem in a way that will allow a solution.

Bertrand Russell

The parties to a dispute have clashing ideas regarding what has happened or what they should do. Once they describe their dispute, the mediator must manage the discussion in a way that does not simply reinforce their differences. She must take the content of what each party has said, rearrange and reshape it, and then get parties to look at this new phenomenon in a structured way. She does so by first identifying and exploring the parties' common interests.

Find Common Interests

In Chapter 7, the idea of *interests* was introduced. As the parties present their concerns, the mediator is listening for interests. Interests are basic human motivators, the underlying needs that drive parties. They include: respect, recognition, reputation, financial stability, freedom, fun, shelter, security, safety, love, control, and health. In many situations parties share an interest in re-establishing control over their lives. Usually, both landlords and tenants want a safe, clean and secure building. Even in the midst of a divorce, both parents usually want a happy childhood for their children. Management and labor share an interest in a thriving business. Normally, neighbors want their environment to be cordial and comfortable. These powerful common interests are often lost sight of in the heat of conflict. If the mediator begins the discussion by extracting the common interests and generating agreement on the large targets for the mediation, the conversation has a goal—securing or advancing the common interests—that can draw parties towards collaboration. The next step is to crystallize the bargaining agenda itself—the issues.

Identify and Frame the Issues

As the mediator listens to each side talk, she distills a series of negotiating issues. Once the parties explore and resolve the issues, they will have resolved their dispute. The sum of the issues comprises the bargaining agenda.

An *issue* is a matter, practice, or action that frustrates or in some way adversely affects a person's interests, goals, or needs. Abortion, for example, is a social issue because its practice adversely affects the goals or interests of some people (for example, interests in freedom and control of one's body, on the one hand, and in furthering religious convictions and preserving life, on the other).

Issues are not facts. Whether abortion, for instance, is a widespread practice or is safe only when practiced by persons with particular training or when performed under particular conditions are factual matters that may be important to a discussion and resolution of the issue, but they are not the issue. To take a less important matter, how the issue of washing the dinner plates is resolved may be affected by the fact of who washed last night's plates—but knowing that fact does not automatically resolve the issue.

A *negotiating issue* is an issue that negotiators—that is, identifiable individuals—are capable of resolving with the resources available to them. Employers and unions can negotiate specific wage standards for themselves, but they cannot resolve the social issue of unemployment. Individual agencies and employees can address issues of employment practices for women and minorities by adopting affirmative action programs and policies, but they cannot resolve the social issues of sexism or racism.

A mediator wants to help parties identify negotiating issues and then focus discussion on them. A helpful way to identify a negotiating issue is to ask: what did one party do to drive the other party crazy? Label that action or practice, and one has just identified a negotiating issue.

People can negotiate about anything: where to eat dinner, what a person's salary should be, what classes to take next semester, where to locate a nuclear power plant. But the bargaining agenda should not be cluttered with topics the disputants cannot resolve.

Example 1. On December 1, three employees of a large corporation in New York City win tickets to attend the Orange Bowl, to be held in Florida on the evening of New Year's Day. The personnel handbook states that all employees are entitled to full pay for eleven designated holidays, one of which is New Year's Day. But the handbook also states that an employee must be present both the day before and the day after the holiday in order to be paid for that holiday. Each employee has used up his allotted vacation time, and it is impossible for anyone to attend the game and return home in time to attend work on January 2. They approach their supervisor and ask to negotiate the issue of holiday pay; they propose that she change the policy so that employees in her department receive pay for holidays as long as they are at work either the day before or the day after the holiday. The negotiating issue of holiday pay, however, cannot be resolved by these parties, as the supervisor does not have the authority to establish policy governing vacation pay.

A mediator must help the parties formulate issues in specific terms. Sometimes parties' discussions flounder not because they disagree about the substance of a matter but because one party literally does not know what the other side wants to discuss.

Example 2. A group of parents registered their concern about their children's low reading scores by conducting a sit-in at their neighborhood elementary school. They demanded to meet with the superintendent of schools. At their first meeting with the superintendent's representative, the parent group presented their list of three issues, as follows: "administrators and administrative performance, teachers and teacher performance, students and student performance." District officials genuinely did not understand what they were being asked to consider. The mediators met with the parent group to distill the negotiating issues of concern to the parents. As a result of those meetings, the parent group submitted another list of issues that pinpointed their concerns: library resources; time allocation between various subjects being taught; incentives for teachers; curriculum in each grade; testing practices; and so on. Three months later, the parties reached an agreement.

Finally, a mediator must promptly translate the issues into language that is nonjudgmental because negotiating parties, in almost every setting, formulate their concerns in accusatory, critical terms that are unhelpful to constructive discussion.

> *Example 3.*
> MONICA: Maria, I can't work on this project with Ritu. She is so inconsiderate. It is freezing cold in our office. She keeps knocking the thermostat down to 60.
> RITU: C'mon. A little fresh air keeps the blood flowing and is good for everyone's health. In fact, we should open the window so people like you wake up.
> MARIA (the boss/mediator): The two of you must complete your project by the end of the day, so I suggest that we figure out quickly how you will deal with the matter of *temperature in your room.*

It seems sensible to identify negotiating issues precisely and label them in neutral language—i.e., in language that does not favor or antagonize any party. The reason it is important for the mediator to do this—and why she makes a significant contribution to resolving disputes in doing so—is that parties often neglect to do it. They are understandably wrapped up in the matter. Frequently, they see only their own concerns and have no patience to listen to the concerns of others. When they talk, they hurl accusations and blame at each other. The mediator's job is to build a structure within which the parties can channel their remarks. From the information that she accumulates, the mediator sorts out the parties' negotiating issues and uses them to build the bargaining agenda. Consider the following information that a mediator learned from the parties and examine how she first identifies common interests and then frames negotiating issues in nonjudgmental terms:

> *Example 4.* Keith Browning is a high school history teacher. The school year has ended and graduation exercises are scheduled for next week. Ann Jackson, a student in Browning's U.S. history class, submitted her term paper two weeks ago, four days after the announced deadline. Browning gave Jackson an "F" for the paper, citing its tardiness as the conclusive reason for his action. When Jackson spoke to Browning about her paper and the grade, he noted that the paper was very well written, unlike papers she had submitted earlier in the term; he strongly hinted that she had plagiarized someone's work in writing the paper. Since Jackson left that meeting, she has been telling her friends that Browning is a racist; graffiti containing similar charges have appeared on walls in the hallways and restrooms. Jackson is a senior in high school; because she

received an "F" on her paper, she will not pass the course, and, since the course is required for graduation, she will not graduate with her class.

Last week, Browning was walking toward his car in the faculty parking lot when he saw Jackson and three of her friends standing by his car. When they saw him, they immediately ran. When Browning reached his car, he noted that the left back tire was slashed and the window on the left side was shattered. The next day, Browning filed a complaint at the neighborhood mediation center, demanding that Jackson pay him $380 for the damage to his car that was caused by her vandalism.

Browning is a fifty-five-year-old white male who has taught at the high school for twenty-four years. Jackson is a seventeen-year-old black female. Her paper was titled "The Biography of Malcolm X." She adamantly claims that she wrote the term paper herself and describes her effort as "the hardest I have ever worked on anything because I was so fascinated by the subject."

First, the mediator would explore common interests. Both Browning and Jackson share an interest in their *reputation* in the school environment. Both share an interest in *respect* and *recognition*—as teacher and student—from one another. And both share an interest in his or her respective *career*. Browning's standing in the school is important to his continuing there as a teacher. Jackson needs a high school diploma for her career. Starting the conversation by acknowledging these interests can remind the parties of what is at stake and of important commonalities they share. Each side's interests have been adversely impacted by one another's actions. But, since each side has the power to do things for the other that can mitigate those impacts, the negotiating issues should be welcome and powerful conversational magnets.

Next, the mediator frames the issues. Here, the mediator's notes might reflect the following issues:

- *Jackson's Term Paper*
    Grade Given the Paper
    Browning's Remarks about the Paper's Quality

- *Comments about Browning*
    Jackson's Statements about Browning to Third Parties
    Graffiti about Browning

- *Damage to Browning's Car*
    The Tire
    The Window

Many of these matters—the remarks made by Browning and Jackson, the graffiti, the treatment of Jackson's paper—affect important interests of both Jackson and Browning. Since they have the power to do something about those issues, the issues are *negotiable*. To put it another way, Jackson and Browning have some degree of control over how their own behavior has affected or could affect each other's reputation and could propose things that each might do for the other that would secure their desired status in their school community (of course, proposing solutions and gaining agreement are two separate tasks). Browning, for instance, might consider giving Jackson a passing mark in his course if she passed a test he would devise for her, or Jackson might propose Browning give her an oral exam on her paper topic in order to prove that she wrote the paper herself and, assuming she passes the exam, then give her a passing grade for the course. Jackson and Browning, if moved by each other's remarks, might apologize to one another. Whether they will or can agree to do any of these things is not yet known, but framing the issues is a first step towards enhancing understanding and creating an environment where resolution is possible.

The mediator must label the negotiating issues not to favor any party. If the mediator were to frame the issue of damage to Browning's car as "vandalism of Browning's car," Jackson would experience that statement as accusatory and might immediately believe that the mediator accepts the teacher's version of events, not hers, and conclude that she is no longer neutral. Alternatively, the mediator does not label Browning's reported statements as "racist assumptions and comments by Browning" as that framing would offend Browning. If the mediator takes sides through her language, the conversational dynamic moves towards attack and defense, as opposed to problem solving.

Note that the issue of "damage to Browning's car," can be discussed without Jackson and Browning reaching any determination about Jackson's involvement. Probably, Jackson will not admit that she damaged the car. Mediated discussions are not a forum in which the primary goal is to make Browning prove beyond a reasonable doubt that Jackson committed the crime of which he accuses her. Browning wants money to repair his car. It is not essential to his getting some money from Jackson that she also admit that she damaged the car; the two elements usually go together, but it is not necessary that they do. If Jackson thought it in her best interest to pay Browning some money for the car even though her friends were the ones who damaged it, she is free to do so. All that is open to negotiation (again with the *caveat* that talking about it and agreeing to it don't always occur together).

Framing the issues is only the first step the mediator takes. She must now determine which negotiating issue she wants the parties to discuss first and the order of all remaining issues. To do that, she must develop a strategic framework for the agenda.

Develop a Bargaining Agenda

We can talk about only one thing at a time. If there are two or more negotiating issues to discuss, we must order the discussion. Who decides what the sequence should be? On what basis do we select a negotiating issue to be first?

The mediator plays an important role in establishing the order in which the negotiating issues are discussed. She must be certain that the parties have provided sufficient information so that she can identify and frame all the negotiating issues. (Remember that a mediator's notes should be limited to recording and labeling interests, negotiating issues, and proposals, rather than the facts. Such notes will be a valuable aid in completing this next step.) From that foundation, the mediator develops a bargaining agenda, governed by one overriding concern: discuss the negotiating issues in the order most likely to result in the parties coming to better understandings and possible resolution of *all* issues. The creation of an agenda takes the dispute from a relatively chaotic jumble of accusations, hurt feelings, and blocked interests to an organized group of topics that the parties can address. A simple, elegant and logical agenda boosts confidence that the dispute may be manageable after all.

A Thoughtful Agenda HELPS!

H ighlight common interests
E asy issues first
　　• Relationship of party to issue
　　• Remedy
L ogical categories and sequence
P riority for pressing deadlines
S tability and balance

A mediator never locks herself into discussing negotiating issue A before negotiating issue B simply because A occurred earlier than B, because A appears before B in a written proposal, or because the parties discussed A before B when they presented their concerns to the mediator. Instead, she reviews all the

matters the parties have raised and makes a quick assessment of how to organize the bargaining agenda.

The mediator applies five organizing principles to structure the agenda. The
agenda, in turn, HELPS disputants to achieve a different perspective of their
dispute and of ways to address it. Each principle provides a basis for helping
the mediator determine the best ordering of the conversation. Once the mediator identifies interests and negotiating issues, she can use the following
guides to order discussion:

Highlight Common Interests

Similar to presenting a purpose clause to introduce a constitution, an agreement, or a law, framing the bargaining agenda by establishing common goals
will pull the parties together. If they can agree on the target, it will be easier
to determine both the obstacles (the issues) and the possible resolutions. In
the example, after a discussion, Browning and Jackson might acknowledge
that they share an interest in respectful treatment and a good reputation.

Easy Issues First

A mediator has the greatest probability for moving discussions forward by
operating on the principles of momentum and investment. Simply stated: discuss first the negotiating issue that the mediator believes will be the easiest for
the parties to resolve. That way, the parties experience success, generate forward momentum, and have something to lose if their talks break down—they
have an investment in the mediation. A mediator wants to get parties to agree
about something, however trivial, so that they have a template for movement
once they get to harder issues. This simple principle does not always govern,
but it should always be considered.

Usually, the easiest negotiating issue to resolve is also the least important to
the parties. Occasionally, a mediator will get lucky and find that the easiest issue
to resolve is also the most important to the parties (for instance, two teenagers
might agree quickly on which weekend evening each one will use the family car,
but disagree about who must chauffeur their parents to the golf course each af-
ternoon so that the car is available for use). Some parties try to resist the mediator's effort to begin with easier, less important issues; they may comment: "We're
wasting our time and fooling no one by talking about those things which have
no effect on settling the really tough matters on which we are miles apart." But
the mediator must persist, explaining the rationale for a thoughtful ordering of
issues. Experience in mediated discussions confirms the following lesson: piercing a party's resistance to change is done most effectively on an incremental basis.

How does a mediator determine which negotiating issue will be the easiest to resolve? There is no foolproof formula for making that decision, but if a mediator decides incorrectly, she will get very rapid feedback from the parties. In deciding what is "easy" to resolve, the mediator might look to:

- *The Relationship of the Parties to the Issue.* The mediator is given a variety of clues regarding the importance of issues to individual parties. The parties, for instance, might display a noticeable vigor while discussing some concerns and exhibit a lack of emotional involvement when mentioning others. They might describe some matters in great detail and spend very little time discussing others. They might use language that indicates varying degrees of commitment to a given item ("I want us to share our parental responsibilities" is more flexible than "I want us to share equally our parental responsibilities"). The mediator must be attuned to listen for these nuances and move rapidly to capitalize on them. Generally, the greater the importance of the issue, the more explosive and difficult it might be to resolve.

  Some parties develop an enormous attachment—emotional, political, philosophical, or personal—to particular issues. A union might announce before collective bargaining sessions begin that its top priority for that round is job security; any management proposal that might jeopardize that interest will be difficult to resolve. A group of corporate board members might have a very strong emotional attachment to providing financial support to a particular local charity because the corporation's deceased founder felt strongly about that charity's work; proposals to eliminate that contribution in favor of another organization will be hotly contested and not easily resolved. The easiest issues to resolve are those from which the parties are most politically and emotionally detached.

- *The Nature of Remedies.* People resolve issues by agreeing to do or not to do something about them. A mediator can compare the issues according to what types of things the parties are being asked to do and evaluate those remedial actions according to two standards:

  1. Mutuality of Exchange. Some negotiating issues can be resolved only if all parties do something for one another: offer an apology or take steps to restore personal reputations that have been tarnished by the dispute. This type of issue might be the easiest to resolve, since all parties start on an equal footing.

  2. Degree of Burden of Compliance. Some negotiating issues can be resolved by one party agreeing to do things that are not too burdensome. The

solutions to other issues might require one party to do things that more dramatically affect its welfare or challenge its fundamental interests. The successful mediator will start with those issues for which the solutions require the least burdensome acts.

Logical Categories and Sequence

The mediator can divide the negotiating issues into various substantive categories, assess which category of issue or issues will be the easiest to resolve, and then channel the initial discussion to that category. She might divide issues into such categories as economic and noneconomic; financial and behavioral; financial support, educational expenses, and parenting responsibilities; political, legal, and administrative; or chronological/reverse chronological development of issues. Different types of disputes call for different categories, and the mediator must always consider whether the issues in dispute can be grouped together in helpful ways. The easiest place to start may be with the negotiating issue that developed first in time, or, alternatively, with the most recent issue. The assumption supporting this strategy is that the mediator can rapidly secure agreement from the parties on the first or last link of the chain of issues. The mediator can then use that agreement to put the remaining matters in context.

Some matters are logically related to one another in the sense that agreement on some issues logically requires agreement on others. A parent and child will not agree on the time at which the child must return from attending the high school football game that night if they disagree over the logically prior issue of whether she will be going out at all. A group of landowners might oppose the proposed relocation of the Appalachian Trail because they fear it will split their land and make it impossible to farm; the mediator must clarify whether the landowners object to the presence of an Appalachian Trail in that area at all, or whether they simply oppose the proposed route.

Structuring the discussion of logically related negotiating issues is a tricky matter for the mediator. In some cases it may be more effective to ignore the logically prior issue and begin discussion on its logical consequent. If a child assures her parent that she will be home within half an hour of the end of the high school football game or 10:00 p.m., whichever is earlier, that specific commitment may help her gain agreement on the issue of whether she can go out at all. This approach can lead to success in negotiation even though the issues, logically speaking, are reversed.

The negotiating issues can also be related causally to one another. By first examining the basic cause of the dispute, the mediator enables everyone to address the remaining issues more constructively. Although beginning mediators are particularly apt to choose this rationale for shaping the discussion of the issues, it is a dangerous strategy that should be used only sparingly and with great caution. The search for "basic" causes is often a spurious enterprise; further, this approach encourages parties to view problem solving as an exercise in establishing guilt or innocence for previous conduct rather than as a joint effort in shaping their future in light of their past—hence, using this approach can result in retarding the settlement-building process rather than accelerating it.

Priority for Pressing Deadlines

Some issues must be resolved by a particular deadline if parties want to avoid potentially more costly or undesired consequences. Other issues don't involve the same time pressure. The easiest issue to resolve normally is the most pressing one, because all parties feel the need to resolve it. If a divorcing couple wants to send their child to private school, they must resolve the issue of tuition payments for that semester even if they have not resolved any other financial arrangements. Failure to resolve it will result in something that both consider undesirable: the child will not attend that particular (or perhaps any) school.

Stability and Balance

In ordering an agenda, the mediator must be aware of the possible impact of choosing an issue of one side first—the other side might feel that the mediator is not neutral. Consequently, where there is an issue of mutual concern, that issue might be discussed first. If the mediator then proposes an issue that is associated with one party next, she could subsequently alternate issues between the parties (e.g., 1. mutual issue; 2. issue of party A; 3. issue of party B . . .).

With these five principles in mind, how might the mediator structure the agenda with Jackson and Browning? While different mediators will make different judgments, the application of these standards might result in reframing, re-grouping and re-ordering the negotiating issues as follows:

1. *Communication*
   Browning's Comments about Jackson's Paper
   Jackson's Statements about Browning to Third Parties
   Graffiti about Browning

Communication is mutual in that each side has issues of concern, so the mediator is not choosing one side over the other by starting here. For two of the issues—*Browning's Comments* and *Jackson's Statements*—refraining from future communications about the other party might be easy to do. It may be that the parties would agree to apologize—a result that would generate good will when tackling the more difficult issues that follow. With respect to the *Graffiti about Browning,* Jackson's possible agreement to refrain from writing graffiti and to ask her friends to do the same does not seem burdensome, as it does not entail her admitting she is responsible for the graffiti in the first place. Even if the parties do not come to agreement, the recognition of mutual harm might provide a perspective shift that would be helpful in addressing other issues.

2. Jackson's Term Paper

In terms of the chronology, this issue "created" the dispute in the first place. Consequently, logic suggests it be addressed early in the agenda. Looked at another way, it may be much easier to resolve matters concerning the term paper than the *Damage to Browning's Car,* particularly if Browning wants Jackson to pay for the damage; there are multiple options that Browning might consider for Jackson, all consistent with his various interests as an educator, if he is motivated to do so.

3. Damage to Browning's Car
    The Tire
    The Window

This is perhaps the most explosive and difficult issue. Placing this issue last gives the parties an opportunity to shift their understanding of each other prior to dealing with it. Also, if there has been positive movement, and consequently "investment" based on some agreements, it may help motivate parties to try harder on this issue. Browning, for example, might forego his monetary demand (perhaps covered by insurance already) or Jackson might agree to some reparations.

By thoughtfully structuring the discussion, the mediator can provide order, optimism and momentum—a breath of fresh air for parties embroiled in controversy. Sometimes the parties will want to control the agenda themselves and bargain over the order of the issues. Even in such cases, the mediator continues to analyze alternative agenda structures so if discussions stall, she is prepared to propose a different tack.

A thoughtful agenda does not guarantee immediate success. Nor does it guarantee that the conversation will proceed in a linear way where the parties resolve one issue before moving to another. Rather, the parties may make progress on one issue, then falter; the mediator must be flexible, move to a different issue, and revisit the unresolved issue at a later time.

The mediator's job is to identify negotiating issues clearly, describe them in non-evaluative language, and control the order of discussion. No one will applaud her for doing this job well, but parties will reach an agreement in spite of, not thanks to, the mediator if she does this part of her job poorly. The "D" of BADGER is both difficult and stimulating because the mediator must make decisions instantaneously. She must gather facts, sort them into negotiating issues using nonjudgmental labels, and measure those negotiating issues against principles in a way that HELPS parties move forward. Then, as soon as the parties have completed their presentations, the mediator, without pause, must say, "Why don't we talk first about _____" and, as she fills in the blank, all these tasks must have been completed.

There is one other reason to emphasize the importance of this dimension of the mediator's role. The parties themselves rarely think about these matters. Understandably, they concentrate on the wrongs they have suffered and getting what they want. But someone—the mediator—must organize and manage the discussion process so that they have an improved chance of succeeding.

The mediator is more than a discussion police officer who simply makes sure people can travel the same road without colliding. The mediator must help create new roads, develop road signs, tune up the parties' discussion engines, and escort the parties on their trip. That is what the "D" component of BADGER—develop the discussion strategy—accomplishes.

But even doing all this does not guarantee that the parties will reach their destination. What does the mediator do when the parties simply disagree about how to resolve the matter that the mediator has so deftly framed and placed in a strategic discussion context? How does a mediator get people to change their minds, modify their proposals, or make concessions so they can move toward agreement?

9

Generate Movement

We can't solve problems by using the same kind of thinking we used when we created them.

Albert Einstein

People often disagree. It is more remarkable how frequently they are able to solve their disagreements. Something happens that enables persons in conflict to strike a deal and move ahead. But what are the factors that break a logjam? What gets someone to change his mind and agree to do something he had previously rejected? The mediator must be conscious of these leverage points and use them to generate movement toward understanding and resolution.

The mediator focuses his efforts in five areas. He (1) examines common interests and ideals, (2) expands the information base, (3) encourages individual perspective-taking, and (4) urges the use of negotiating norms and practices. If those fail, he (5) appeals to the big picture. Each target area contains leverage points.

Common Interests and Ideals

Common interests are interwoven into the discussion as each new issue is addressed. If a party could get what he wanted without the cooperation of others, he would have no need to appreciate the interests of others or to expose his own. Most people cooperate voluntarily only if they are convinced that they are not sacrificing their own interests. To gain the cooperation of the other side, the proposed deal must address the interests and ideals of one's counterpart. A mediator can persuade parties to do things by pointing out how proposed settlement terms promote mutual goals rather than reinforce one party's gain at another's expense.

1. *Highlight interdependence.* Everyone wants to win. But the goal of mediated discussions is not for any one party to win. Rather, it is for all parties to develop a shared view of their problem so that they can solve it to their mutual satisfaction. The mediator emphasizes the reality that one party's ability to achieve its objective depends on securing the freely granted cooperation of others; gaining that cooperation requires that each party believe it will be no worse off after accepting the proposed settlement terms than it was before the discussions began. That does not mean that power relationships among the parties do not affect outcomes, or that there is no room in mediated discussions for "tough negotiators." Far from it. But parties must wield their power for some purpose, and the mediator must remind the disputants that using their power to prevail over others is not as effective as using it to get what they need.

2. *Identify joint or shared interests.* When parties to a conflict become preoccupied with getting what they want or piercing the other's obstinacy, they often forget that they have joint interests. An employee and his supervisor have a common interest in a cordial, or at least functional, working relationship. Divorcing business partners have a shared interest in their reputation and careers surviving the split-up intact. Most disputants have a common interest in minimizing the costs of disputing. A mediator must develop and repeatedly remind the parties of their shared needs.

3. *Appeal to commonly held principles.* Disputants can usually agree on general principles. It's their application—the specifics—that creates the controversy. A mediator wants to make sure that parties realize they can agree on something, and he can best accomplish that by getting parties to agree on principles. These principles might be simple guidelines: "Can we all agree that we will not interrupt each other or use disrespectful language during our discussions?" or "Can you agree that it is better to try to work out this problem among yourselves rather than have someone else [boss, judge, parent] tell you what you must do?" They might reflect fundamental moral concerns: "Can you agree that it is wrong to inflict pain intentionally on innocent persons?" The goal of these appeals is identical: to get parties to agree to a principle or guideline that has some bearing, however indirect, on resolving the matters in dispute.

4. *Call for a vision of the ideal.* Disputants can sometimes agree on what an ideal relationship should be between business partners, employees, parents, neighbors, landlords and tenants, and nations. The vision of the ideal then

becomes a target in working out the specifics to achieve it. In expressing the ideal, parties often feel stronger and are pleasantly surprised by commonalities.

5. *Emphasize trust-building dimensions of conduct.* Conflicts erode trust among people, and that loss of trust leads them to demand burdensome settlement terms for fear that any less demanding an arrangement will be exploited. A parent does not want her ex-spouse to visit their young children because she does not trust his claim that he has cured his alcoholism; the customer wants his money back rather than having the product repaired because he has no faith that the machine will ever work as advertised. The mediator must get parties to do things for each other that help restore a sense of trust. These gestures need not be dramatic; there is no quick fix to rebuild a person's confidence in another's reliability. But if parties can demonstrate their ability to comply with agreed-on terms, then that conduct serves to restore the credibility of their word, so that a more confident, less regimented relationship can develop thereafter.

6. *Agree on a process for resolving the dispute.* If parties are unable to resolve any of the substantive negotiating issues through mediated discussions, then the mediator should get them to consider whether they can agree on a different process for resolving their dispute. A feuding couple might agree to seek marriage counseling; a landlord and tenant might agree to resolve their controversy in court; businesses divided by contractual issues might agree to a speedy arbitration process; or parties involved in a personal injury lawsuit might agree to engage a neutral expert for an opinion. By helping disputants establish what the next step will be, the mediator helps them stabilize their relationship for a foreseeable period of time—a contribution whose value should not be minimized.

Information

People often change their mind with new information. A mediator is interested in two things: what people know and what they don't. He wants to use both dimensions to move the parties toward agreement. A mediator cannot become too preoccupied with establishing facts, for that can lead to a paralysis of action; but neither can he ignore facts. A mediator wants to get people to agree to do things; new information often triggers new ideas for possible action.

1. *Facts persuade, so develop them.* If an employer resists granting a raise because he believes it costs too much, then figure out what the real cost will be.

Maybe it won't be that expensive, and he will change his mind. If parents are afraid to let a child leave the house at night because they don't know where he will be or with whom, they should find out. They may be less reluctant to let him go if he is participating in a supervised school play than if he plans to hang out on the street corner waiting for some action. Using a calculator in a mediation session to understand the numbers, urging that parties explore the internet to develop options while they wait for their caucus with the mediator, making calls to expand a negotiator's authority, examining documents and pictures that parties bring—all can lead to movement.

2. *Use the absence of facts to create doubts about what has happened or what can happen.* If a landlord cannot establish with a reasonable degree of certainty that his tenant's child hit a baseball through another tenant's window, then the mediator can use that uncertainty to prod him to reduce his demand from full payment for the broken window to assurances that the child not play baseball in the backyard.

3. *Use inconsistent statements to narrow the problem.* If a person complains that his neighbor disturbs him "twenty-four hours a day" by blasting a sound system, but later informs the mediator that he leaves for work every day at 7:30 a.m. and returns home at 6:30 p.m., then the complaining party is not being consistent. The mediator uses that inconsistency not to label the person a liar but to help clarify the problem: it is not a problem of loud music twenty-four hours a day, but one of the volume during those periods when both are home— thirteen hours a day at the most. Subtract another seven hours for the amount of time both people sleep (at the same time, one hopes) and the mediator has narrowed the problem from twenty-four hours to six.

4. *Examine past practices.* Suppose an employee protests his firing for the theft of a seventy five cent candy bar. The amount in question might seem in- significant. But if the employer's past practice has always been to fire employ- ees for theft of company property, regardless of the amount in question, then the mediator might cite that practice in an effort to persuade the employee to drop his protest.

5. *Challenge assumptions.* People assume many things. They assume other people are rich because of the clothes they wear or the cars they drive. They assume the report was filed late because "Jones never hands anything in on time." They assume "all grievances can be resolved with an increased paycheck." The mediator must challenge all assumptions; an erroneous assumption may be blocking an agreement.

6. *Explore feelings.* Feelings are facts. It is important to understand the par- ties' feelings for at least two reasons. First, as powerful motivators, feelings can

be tapped to energize parties to change. For example, suppose siblings are fighting over the disposition of family heirlooms; one sister expresses how much she misses her brothers and sisters and the warmth and fun they used to share. The sister's feelings of love and loss may motivate her to do things for her siblings. Second, feelings are fluid. If parties express their feelings, and the feelings are understood and recognized, the feelings themselves may change. Even if feelings do not change, being heard and understood may itself generate positive feelings by providing recognition and connection. Restoring emotional balance might allow a party to adopt a more flexible approach.

Perspective

Since parties to a mediation do not have to agree, a mediator, in trying to advance resolution, must help them re-examine their perspectives and positions. He does so not only by convincing them that proposed solutions are consistent with their interests, but also by using a series of maneuvers that psychologically position the parties for agreement. Here are some standard techniques that a mediator uses to alter a party's attitude. The mediator must remember that any technique is effective only when used sparingly and sincerely.

1. *Allow for choice.* When parties become locked into a volley of bitter and biting exchanges, an escalating cycle can generate more and more damage. A mediator might ask, "Would you like to continue this conversation about who is at fault—a conversation you have been having for a long time—or do you want to see if we can resolve the issue of _____?" Simply laying out the choice sometimes empowers parties to move in a different direction.

2. *Stroke 'em.* Everyone likes to be complimented. A mediator must reinforce positive behavior by reminding parties that their willingness to mediate, to listen to one another, to come up with proposals, and to "hang in" after (sometimes) many hours of emotional discussion is commendable. When people are praised, they feel stronger. When they are stronger, they are more responsive to others and more creative. To the extent parties are doing a good job, tell them so!

3. *Cite examples with which people can identify.* A mediator must teach and persuade by using vivid examples. To be persuasive, examples must be relevant to, or understandable in the context of, a disputant's individual experience. The mediator who must prod an autocratic manager to work more productively with his free-spirited subordinates is more effective if he cites

examples of differing managerial styles portrayed in episodes of a popular television series than if he appeals to the published findings of social science research regarding leadership behavior.

4. *Use humor.* Laughing makes people feel comfortable with themselves and their surroundings. It breaks the tension and helps put matters into perspective. A mediator should not use a mediated discussion as an opportunity to polish a comedy routine, but he should not hesitate to inject a humorous remark into the discussions. The only *caveats* are obvious: the mediator must be sure that everyone gets the joke and the joke must not be at the expense of any party.

5. *Try role reversal.* Sometimes a party will change his position or better appreciate a particular demand of the other party if the mediator gets him to analyze the negotiating issue from the other party's viewpoint. A teenager might resist obeying his parents' curfew rules because he believes they are unduly restrictive; but a mediator might get him to reconsider his resistance by making the teenager put himself in his parents' shoes and view curfew rules as safety measures developed by persons with an only child living in a high-crime neighborhood.

6. *Exploit peer pressure.* Sometimes a person changes his mind because he does not want to be the only individual in the group who disagrees with the proposed solution. A mediator should capitalize on that need to belong by being sure that the lone party is exposed to the group opinion.

7. *Let silence ring.* Everyone is afraid of silence. A mediator cannot be. People feel awkward when no one is speaking. A mediator must not rush to fill the air with chatter. Silence can bring opportunity. Sometimes one party will relieve the uncomfortable atmosphere by suggesting a possible change in what he is willing to do. The mediator should recognize that movement and explore its possibilities.

8. *Focus on the future, not the past.* A mediator helps parties shape their future. Past events influence that design. But the mediator must remember that no one can change what has happened and that the impact of past events becomes less dominant as their details become ambiguous and disputed. A mediator must not let the parties' competing visions of their past paralyze them.

Suppose a subordinate and his supervisor disagree over whether the supervisor had clearly established the performance objectives that he is now penalizing the subordinate for not meeting. A mediator generates flexibility by expanding the discussion from a contest over what happened or who is at fault to a consideration of the future. Clearly, that discussion will be tempered by their respective beliefs about what occurred; each will propose solutions designed to ensure that similar disputes do not occur. That is fine. A mediator does not want parties to ignore their past; he just wants to be certain they do not become prisoners of it.

9. *Prohibit greed.* In some discussions, one party seems to obtain its favored position on nearly every negotiating issue. At that point, pride creeps in. "I'm on a roll" goes the familiar refrain, and nothing—not even an agreement that gives the party what he needs—will stop it. A mediator must put the brakes on such behavior by reminding that party of how reciprocity and an outcome that benefits both sides can result in compliance with commitments.

10. *Exploit vulnerabilities.* Disputants tend to see things in all-or-nothing terms: "I'm right, you're wrong." One party often insists that only others do what is necessary to correct the situation because they caused the problem. But no one is infallible; everyone has reasons for regret. These lapses constitute vulnerabilities, which the mediator should expose in order to rebalance the discussion. By highlighting vulnerabilities, he emphasizes joint responsibility for the problem and the need for mutual, not unilateral, action to solve it.

11. *Help save face.* Face-saving means maintaining one's dignity or reputation. Everyone says and does things they later regret. Everyone, from time to time, takes positions that are ill-considered. It is rare, however, for people to admit they were wrong or short-sighted. If a mediator can help a party to change positions without looking bad, then movement is far more likely. Sometimes a small concession, a statement of appreciation, or an apology from one side can allow the other side to make a big move without losing face. The mediator must frame the exchange so that the party making the big move does not feel exposed. "Trevor, you say you are willing to give Ashley the house now that she recognizes the extraordinary efforts you made over the years to repair and renovate it." Sometimes, parties will be willing to accept a deal if the proposal appears to come from the mediator rather than from either of the parties. What constitutes acceptable face-saving will be different in every case.

Negotiating Practices

A mediator helps people find acceptable solutions. In moving towards that end, he can avoid impasses by insisting that parties adopt accepted negotiation practices and standards.

1. *Help parties establish priorities.* Parties who assert that every issue is equally significant are either posturing or lack a clear idea of their own interests. Some objectives are more important than others. People make choices by how they act, if not by what they say. A mediator must look for a party's priorities, even

if the party does not explicitly rank them.

2. *Develop trade-offs.* Negotiations are a series of exchanges. Parties exchange things only if they believe the items are of roughly comparable worth. However, given items that are roughly comparable according to the internal calculus of each party, individuals may value them differently. Exchanges are built on these differing valuations. Some individuals value time more than money—they would prefer a smaller payment now to a larger payment next week. Some value relationships more than possessions—they would trade an apology for a decrease in what they are paid. That is why priorities must be established before trade-offs are made. Often the mediator will help parties create an acceptable framework: "If A and B are resolved within certain parameters, then will you be willing to do X in order to resolve C?"

3. *Compel parties to acknowledge constraints.* No one will agree to do something that is the equivalent of suicide, and no negotiating party should expect its counterpart to accept a proposal that has that effect. A business, for example, cannot sell its goods or services below cost for an extended period of time and expect to survive. A mediator must remind parties that their negotiating proposals must not only reflect their own aspirations but also fall within the resource capacity of their negotiating counterparts.

4. *Pursue compromises.* One word that gives mediation a bad name is *compromise.* Many people think that a mediator insists that parties compromise—often interpreted as "split it in half"—to reach a settlement. Unfortunately, compromise carries the stigma of "selling out." This attitude can stand in the way of optimal outcomes. Sometimes compromising is the most desirable alternative. Without using the word "compromise," a mediator encourages parties to do that by urging them to compare what they are getting in return for accepting something less than their desired solution, and to determine whether the exchange is acceptable. There is nothing sinister about that; no one's fundamental interests are necessarily curtailed. A mediator helps parties get what they need, not always what they want.

5. *Look for integrative solutions.* Sometimes people do not have to give up anything to reach a resolution. Suppose there are two furnished, unoccupied offices; one is a large office in the interior section of the office suite, the other a small corner office with a view of the town's park. Two co-workers each demand the corner office. The supervisor brings them together to discuss the matter. He learns that one employee wants the corner office so that he can put his plants on the window ledge where they will flourish in the natural light, whereas the other actually prefers a larger office but wants the desk that is now situated in the corner office. They can resolve the question of office assign-

ment without either having to give up anything. Solutions like this are not readily available for every negotiating issue, but they do sometimes exist, and the mediator must encourage parties to look for them.

6. *Use brainstorming.* Movement is prompted by parties imagining possibilities. A mediator can use brainstorming to get a range of ideas on the table. The mediator invites parties to throw out as many ideas as possible without worrying whether the ideas are good or bad. The mediator captures the ideas—on a flip chart perhaps—without attributing them to a particular party and without judgment. Separating idea-creation from idea-adoption frees people to be creative. Sometimes a bad idea generates a good idea.

"Out of the Box" Thinking

Can you change this figure to the number 6 using no more than one line?
The line can be straight or curved

IX

There are many solutions* to this problem. Identify the "box" you are in when you look at the figure and try to solve the problem using another perspective.

---

* You could place the letter "S" in front of the figure to make "SIX." You could place 6 after the figure to make "IX6." You could fold the figure in half and rotate it 180 degrees; you would have "VI".

---

7. *Prohibit escalating demands.* Once a party proposes a solution, the mediator must insist that he not try to improve it later on. Assume that a personnel officer offers a job to an applicant. They discuss and agree on all aspects of the job and non-salary employment benefits. When the personnel officer asks the applicant about his salary requirements, the candidate states: "I'm looking for a $60,000 annual salary." The personnel officer replies: "That's fine. We have a deal. I'll confirm our arrangements in writing." Then the candidate says: "On reflection, I really need $65,000 to make it worthwhile for me to make this job move." When a negotiating party escalates his demand, it shifts

the target for agreement; such shifting makes resolution impossible because one never knows what it will take to strike a deal. Trust is eroded. A mediator must not let parties negotiate in this fashion because part of the mediator's job is to stabilize expectations. To do so, he must discourage any attempt by a negotiating party to improve its position by increasing its original proposals or resurrecting an earlier proposal that it has since relinquished.

8. *Help orchestrate the dance.* For some negotiators, a negotiation begins with extreme demands and proceeds through a series of incremental moves towards a a mutually-acceptable point. The mediator can facilitate this "dance" in several ways: by helping parties explore whether there is some overlap—a zone of agreement—in what they may be willing to do, by conveying offers in a way that does not antagonize either side, and by trying to shift the discussion so that parties will reveal underlying interests and develop responsive trade-offs.

9. *Use the agenda.* Sometimes when people are stuck, doing something entirely different helps. A problem looks different in the morning when one is fresh and energetic, than it looks at the end of the day. If we make progress on issue A, then issue B might be easier. Consequently, flexibility with the agenda is helpful. When a discussion gets stuck, shelving a particular matter and shifting the focus elsewhere can generate movement and optimism.

10. *Develop time constraints.* People reach decisions under the pressure of deadlines. Union and management negotiate seriously in the face of a strike deadline. Co-workers resolve disagreements over the format of a company publication as the printer's deadline approaches. Some parties resolve lawsuits as the courtroom door opens. The lesson in each case is the same: for all mediated discussions, there is a time period within which the parties have the power to resolve matters by themselves; once that time has elapsed, new and unpredictable forces intervene to affect or determine the result. Parties become less resistant to settlement as they confront the reality of relinquishing control over their fate to those other forces. A mediator uses deadlines to encourage parties to take responsibility for managing their future.

The mediator deploys these levers to generate movement. If by themselves or in combination they do not succeed, then the mediator appeals to his final target.

The Big Picture: The Costs of Not Settling

When people become overwhelmed by failed attempts to resolve a dispute, they may become impatient, self-righteous and shortsighted. This is not dishonorable; it is a common experience. But it does not help us resolve conflict. It is up to the mediator to remind the parties of a simple fact: obstinacy has a price tag. There are consequences if mediation is not successful. The mediator's job is to force the parties to compare those consequences with the proposed solutions they can freely adopt. For this tactic to be effective, the mediator must use it sparingly. He must portray the cost comparison two ways.

1. *Quality-of-life costs.* What happens if the parties don't resolve their problem? People must alter their life-styles to deal with the unresolved problem. Morale can plummet, people brood, and performance deteriorate; annoyance can fester and resentment build. These can be the real consequences of living with an unresolved problem. The mediator must ask the parties: Do you prefer this over the proposed settlement? If not, then develop an acceptable solution; if yes, there will be no mediated agreement.

This appeal is the most powerful tool in the mediator's kit. He must accurately relate the costs of not settling to the realities of the disputants' situation. He must not be misleading or overdramatic, but he should describe the potential situation with an artistry that vividly captures the human cost of continued impasse. His description must remind the parties of how they rely on each other's conduct to secure their own satisfaction. After that, he can let the parties make their choice.

2. *Process costs.* If mediated discussions collapse, parties will use alternative procedures to resolve their dispute. Minimally, this means that more time will elapse before they resolve their situation. Some procedures may require expending additional resources as well; if a person chooses to resolve a contested employment discharge in court rather than accept proposed settlement terms, he will incur additional legal fees and lose time from work (and possibly wages) to attend the court sessions. Often, litigation takes months—or years—to conclude. Depending on the alternative people choose, they may be required to abide by someone else's determination of how the dispute should be resolved. These are the tangible costs that parties incur if they prefer continued impasse to accepting the proposed settlement terms. The mediator must describe these to the parties—and then let them decide what they want to do.

A mediator uses many tools to persuade parties to move forward without any guarantee that a particular effort will work. Some issues will be resolved easily and without controversy; others will be more difficult. A mediator's personal experience and knowledge of human behavior will guide him in knowing when to increase the pressure, when to relent, and when to return for the final push to settlement.

The mediator must not be deterred from employing every appeal possible to badger the parties to understand their situation fully, to be creative in developing options and to come to terms of agreement. He must not feel badly about pushing a party to reconsider and reevaluate positions the party appears reluctant to change; if a party does not want to settle, he has the freedom to decline. The mediator's job is to help the parties reach an agreement, not to win a popularity contest. His job is to encourage movement, persistently and energetically.

Generating movement is the heart of the mediator's work, the culmination of everything he has done—beginning the discussion, accumulating information, and developing the discussion agenda—because the goal of those efforts is to establish a context in which persuasion can occur. Trying to do this is intellectually challenging and emotionally exhausting. It is what makes mediating an intensely rewarding experience.

Mediators use one specific procedure to generate movement that requires separate analysis. This procedure—meeting separately with the parties—combines in microcosm all the discussion strategies and persuasive techniques already analyzed. It is the one mediation procedure that constitutes our conventional image of "shuttle diplomacy." The procedure operates on different psychological and strategic premises from those discussed previously. In many contexts, mediated discussions can proceed with all parties present all the time; the mediator directs discussion, clarifies communication, encourages candor, and tries to move parties toward agreement in everyone's presence. At times, however, a mediator may believe that progress toward agreement will come—that is, persuasion will be effective—only by talking alone with individual parties. On what basis a mediator makes that decision and how he conducts these individual meetings are matters we must now consider.

10

ELECT Separate Sessions

The biggest problem with communication is the illusion it has occurred.
George Bernard Shaw

A mediator chooses to meet separately with the parties—to caucus with them—because she believes that doing so will contribute to understanding and settlement. A caucus allows the mediator to obtain information and insights and impart information and encourage insights privately that a mediator does not believe can occur—or occur constructively—in joint discussions.

A caucus can take place individually with each of several parties and the mediator. Or, the mediator might meet with different subsets of participants. In a case involving construction defects, separate meetings with the general contractor, the architect, and multiple subcontractors might be constructive. In a case involving teenagers and their parents, the mediator might meet separately with the parents and the teenagers. Sometimes the parties need to meet privately—or caucus—with their own team without the mediator. Whichever configuration is used, the benefit of caucusing is the possibility that different insights and opportunities are sparked by working in different groupings.

Caucusing is another tool for a mediator. As with any tool, she must know why, when, and how to use it.

Why and When to Caucus

There are both psychological and strategic reasons to use a caucus. Some persons are willing to share information, insights, and aspirations with the mediator as long as others do not hear what they say. Such behavior is common:

a child shares information with one parent about the other parent only on the condition that it remain confidential; students share feelings with deans about a particular professor, but not in that professor's presence; subordinates communicate concerns about their boss to colleagues or resource personnel which they do not reveal to their boss. People's motives for behaving this way are complex, ranging from not wanting to hurt themselves, to not wanting to offend the person who is the subject of their remarks. By meeting in a caucus, a mediator can build on this reality and perhaps gather information that will help resolve the dispute.

If people trust the mediator, they share a remarkable range of information during these separate sessions. They indicate priorities among the issues, the range of their flexibility with respect to how particular matters can be resolved, the extent of their resources, their personal aspirations or hidden agenda, the political problems they face with those they represent, or the bitterness they harbor toward the particular persons with whom they are meeting. Sometimes parties will readily strike an agreement without ever sharing—or feeling the need to share—such information with the mediator. At other times, when the parties are making no progress, the mediator must acquire such information to help forge an agreement, and the only way she can get it is by caucusing.

People also have a psychological need for a safety zone during discussions. They need time to consider ideas, evaluate what others have said, and brainstorm solutions without feeling pressured into making an immediate response or being locked in by what they say. They need a chance to make tentative commitments without fear that others will interpret such remarks as definitive concessions: "Well, but if I did that, would she be willing to do this?" By meeting in a caucus session, a mediator creates this safety zone for each participant.

Once people are in a dispute, trust among them erodes. When this happens, they become skeptical about what the other person says or offers. They lose their capacity to objectively evaluate ideas that the other side puts forward. A caucus with a mediator can counter this phenomenon by the mediator discussing a proposal or encouraging its examination in a less tense environment where its advantages can be explored and perhaps embraced.

A mediator must chip away at each party's rigidity. Sometimes the only way to generate flexibility is by asking a series of probing—sometimes leading—questions that expose vulnerability. The danger of doing that in everyone's presence is threefold: first, the mediator will generate a defensive response that will reinforce the parties' differences and make the attacked party "dig in" to save face; second, she will undercut the parties' perception of the mediator's neutrality; finally, if the other parties witness the mediator engaged in such an attack, they may think she has now become their advocate, and may begin to believe that they do not need to modify their own position. By asking such questions in a caucus format, however, the mediator avoids these pitfalls.

> *Example 1.* A dissatisfied customer states that her $750 suit was irreparably damaged while being handled by employees at the dry cleaner; she demands full reimbursement for a new suit. The storeowner claims that the damage consisted only of a slight tear in the jacket sleeve, which her tailor had repaired; as a "sign of good will," however, the storeowner offers to settle the matter by giving the customer a "token amount" of credit toward future dry cleaning charges. Both parties hold firm. At some point the mediator must ask the customer directly whether she is willing to accept less money in order to reach a settlement. But if the parties have been adamant in their positions up to that point, then the mediator knows that the answer to this question will be a resounding "no." So she must not ask it in everyone's presence. If the mediator asks either party that question in a caucus, however, in conjunction with a penetrating review of the costs of not settling, she might trigger a different response.

A mediator wants parties to recognize unattractive settlement alternatives and weaknesses in their positions. Insights about poor alternatives and vulnerabilities can generate flexibility and settlement proposals. The challenge becomes highlighting such weaknesses without making a party feel that the mediator has turned against her and without advantaging the other side. The mediator escapes both horns of that dilemma by pursuing the analysis in separate meetings.

So a mediator has sound bases for meeting separately with the parties. She need not feel locked into conducting all discussions in everyone's presence. But she must recognize that meeting separately creates special obligations and challenges.

Both the timing of a caucus session and the choice of whom to meet with first are dictated by the purpose the mediator wants to promote. These general purposes are captured by the pneumonic ELECT: expand the information base and settlement options (E); lessen intransigence (L); encourage evaluation (E); confirm movement (C); and take a "time-out" (T).

ELECT: To Meet Separately with the Parties

E:	Expand information base and settlement options.
L:	Lessen intransigence.
E:	Encourage evaluation.
C:	Confirm movement.
T:	Take a "time-out."

Expand the Information Base and Settlement Options

Some parties will simply not share certain critical information in front of their negotiating counterpart. When the mediator develops a feeling that there is an important piece of the story missing, a caucus might help to provide it. In this case, meeting first with the party who is mysteriously reticent makes sense.

In other cases, after some period of time, parties engaged in joint discussion begin to repeat themselves; they reject all proposed solutions. The mediator must gain a better understanding of why particular options are unacceptable. She must provide an atmosphere in which parties can explore possible solutions without exposing their flexibility or having to make an immediate decision. She calls for a caucus. From a substantive viewpoint, it does not matter which party the mediator meets with first. The mediator's choice is frequently guided by such considerations as which party is seeking to alter the *status quo* or which party believes itself to be at an emotional, political, or power disadvantage; meeting first with those persons is frequently interpreted by them as bestowing a sense of legitimacy and equality with other participants that might put them at ease and encourage flexibility.

Lessen Intransigence

At some point in the discussions, a mediator knows that someone must change her position on a specific issue to advance settlement. Suppose the owner of the dry cleaning store, in the earlier example, informs the mediator after a lengthy discussion that she will pay no more than $100 to her dissatisfied customer; to pay any more, in her judgment, would make the cost of settlement exceed any costs she might incur in not settling. The customer vehemently rejects this offer as "insulting" and demands payment in full for a new suit. The mediator senses that both parties have dug in. She must try to convince the customer to accept less than full payment and the owner to pay something more than $100—or both. The mediator attempts to change the customer's position not because she believes the customer is wrong in maintaining it or thinks the store owner's offer is a fair settlement; she does so because she is convinced there will be no agreement unless someone moves. In caucus, the mediator forcefully explores the costs of continued recalcitrance—the risk of losing at trial or in arbitration, the loss of a valuable relationship, the aggravation of having the matter unresolved, the possible reputational costs, and so on.

Parties miscalculate how their conduct affects others. They misread or are oblivious to people's reactions to their bargaining demands, language, or behavior. The mediator must address those situations. A mediator, of course, does not have to wait to be told that certain conduct is deeply offensive and will polarize discussions. If she sees that one party's conduct is alienating others, then she can separate the parties and speak privately with the offending party.

> *Example 2.* In the middle of a budget negotiation, one party accused the other of "killing innocent children by denying youth programs a larger share of the available monies." The mediator called for a caucus and met first with the budget director. The first words of the caucus exploded out of the budget director's mouth: "If that s.o.b. accuses me again of being a child killer, I'm going to lose it and end these discussions." Before returning to the joint session, the mediator spoke with the accusing party and forcefully warned her that the consequence of making such charges would be the collapse of negotiations.

Encourage Evaluation

A mediator needs time to evaluate the progress of the discussions and to design a plan of action. Although she should keep such recesses to a minimum, she must not hesitate to declare one if the need arises. When asking for time to reflect, she indicates to the parties that she is calling for a recess to review her notes and evaluate how best to proceed; she invites them to do the same. The mediator needs to provide a place where each party can be alone or can meet with colleagues, expert advisors or support persons.

In other cases, the mediator plays an important role in sparking a more thorough evaluation of matters by parties in an atmosphere where they are not emotionally crippled by reactions of or to the other side. Hearing an idea or challenge framed by the mediator—even if it originated with the other side— might allow a more dispassionate analysis of its merits.

Confirm Movement

Parties signal a change of position in many ways. Some are explicit: "We have a new wage proposal for you: we are now offering a 4 percent wage increase for each year of the contract." Other shifts are subtle. The proposal that "Every community group that uses the school facilities must assume primary responsibility for cleaning up" becomes "Every community group that uses the school facilities must assume responsibility for cleaning up when it is finished." Sometimes a party signals movement simply by no longer talking about an issue it had raised earlier in the discussion. A mediator who wants to be certain the movement is real rather than an oversight can declare a caucus and meet first with the party that appears to have made the change.

Take a "Time-Out"

Parties need time to consider comments and proposals and reconsider their own position. They need to make decisions without the pressure of an adversary in the room—they need to escape to their safety zone. It may be helpful to have the mediator with them; they may need time to reflect on their own; or they may need to contact someone outside of the discussion. The mediator might declare a caucus after one party has made a new proposal, when someone seems overwrought, or as the parties are approaching stalemate. She indicates to them the specific topics that she wants each to consider in their separate meetings with the mediator, in their "time out," or while they are waiting for their turn to caucus with the mediator. The meeting or period for reflection is structured substantively and has a time limit. Such a regrouping can result in renewed stamina and momentum.

A mediator who calls for a caucus but cannot identify its general purpose is abusing this valuable tool. A mediator should ELECT to caucus only if separate meetings constitute the most likely avenue for helping the parties move towards consensus.

How to Conduct a Caucus

While each caucus has an identifiable purpose, three principles shape the way a mediator conducts it:

1. All discussions are confidential unless the party authorizes the mediator to share their content.

2. The mediator meets with every party each time she calls for a caucus.
3. The amount of time a mediator spends with each party in a caucus need not be identical.

Within this framework, a mediator proceeds as follows. The mediator indicates to all parties that she wants to meet with them separately. She states the order in which she will talk with them (discussing the decision with the parties to avoid perceptions of favoritism), indicates the approximate length of time she will spend with each party (or each group), and excuses everyone but the party with whom she will meet. The party being excused should be given a comfortable waiting area, ideally with a telephone and computer, so she can be collecting her thoughts, obtaining necessary information and developing ideas.

In every caucus the mediator immediately does two things: first, she notes the starting time of the caucus session; second, she organizes her notes so that she separates the information she acquires during a separate session from that obtained during the joint meetings. The reasons for doing these are obvious: first, time goes very rapidly when conducting a caucus, so what seems like fifteen minutes to a mediator may actually be forty-five minutes. The mediator must remember that time passes slowly for parties who are waiting. She must be vigilant not to exceed the time stated. Parties left waiting too long can leave! Second, organizing her caucus notes helps a mediator pinpoint which party knows what at any point in time, thereby facilitating both her own pledge to respect the confidentiality of information gained in the caucus and her capacity to capitalize on the information gap among the parties.

The mediator starts every caucus by stating that the discussion is confidential; she will not share any information with the others unless the party authorizes her to do so. But the mediator also targets the goals of the discussion—e.g. to expand possible settlement options—in order to minimize the possibility that the conversation simply becomes a gossip session.

By the time the mediator completes that statement, she must not only know what she wants to learn in this particular caucus but also have developed a plan for getting it. And the mediator's plan combines strategies for developing a discussion agenda with persuasive strategies for generating movement.

Consider the following scenario:

> *Example 3.* XYZ Corporation manufactures jet engine components for military aircraft. Ales Chernitski and Zahid Chen, skilled mechanics who work next to each other at XYZ's plant, approach their supervisor. Chernitski accuses Chen of intentionally damaging the

tools in his personal tool kit; he demands full reimbursement. Chen accuses Chernitski of creating a hostile work environment by incessantly making racial slurs; in addition, he charges Chernitski with recklessly endangering his safety by intentionally distracting Chen just as he is drilling grooves that require extraordinary precision. Both agree that they should not continue to work next to each other, and each demands that the other be reassigned to work the second shift.

Chen has worked at XYZ Corporation for six years, the last two as a mechanic; Chernitski has worked his entire five-year tenure at XYZ Corporation as a mechanic. The supervisor decides to meet separately with each employee; she talks with Chernitski first. Her purpose is to learn whether there are any circumstances under which Chernitski is willing to work the second shift. What should she talk about with Chernitski, and which issues should she discuss first?

The Initial Caucus Session

Depending on the personalities of Chernitski and Chen as well as the general tenor of the discussion, the supervisor could develop a discussion plan around any of the following starting points:

1. *Chernitski's issue—damaged tools:* This seems to concern Chernitski the most. The supervisor's strategy in starting here is to put Chernitski at ease by demonstrating she has heard that. Even if there is no immediate resolution of that matter, Chernitski will at least feel comfortable in knowing that the supervisor understands what he wants. Then the supervisor can press hard in trying to generate flexibility on the matter of the shift assignments; she has improved her chance for success because the previous discussion has left dangling the possibility of a trade-off on reimbursement for the tools in exchange for agreement to a change in work shifts.

2. *Areas of vulnerability—seniority:* If Chernitski is arrogant or trying to blame Chen for their predicament, then the supervisor might want to equalize the parties by immediately discussing those issues whose resolution could block Chernitski from having his interests met. Following this strategy, the supervisor would begin by discussing the issue of shift assignments and would point out to Chernitski that company policy favors making shift assignments, all other things being equal, on the basis of company-wide seniority, not department-based seniority. Fearing that he might be assigned to that second shift, Chernitski might indicate a willingness to work that shift if Chen reimburses him for the damaged tools.

3. *Areas of mutual interest—safety measures:* Both men agree that they should not continue to work next to each other. Having established that someone will move, but deferring discussion about who will move, and when, the supervisor can have Chernitski identify what he and Chen can do in the immediate future to prevent property damage and ensure their physical safety. The supervisor might then discuss the matter of the damaged tools. With Chernitski obtaining some sense of security in these two areas, the supervisor can then probe the matter of changing one person's shift assignment by discussing first its timing (next week? after this specific project is completed in one month?) and then whose shift will change.

4. *General principles—value of positive work environment.* The supervisor could begin by discussing basic principles that are probably non-controversial: the need to treat each other with respect and not endanger each other's personal safety or property. Each side is likely to endorse the notion that a positive work environment is critical given the sensitive nature of their responsibilities. With those commitments as the frame of reference, the supervisor could then pursue one of the aforementioned strategies.

5. *Costs of not settling—loss of job:* The supervisor might try to create an atmosphere of urgency by immediately reminding Chernitski of what will happen if there is no agreement on who will work the second shift: no reimbursement for the damaged tools, possible disciplinary actions against both Chernitski and Chen, and a unilateral decision by the supervisor as to which shift each person will work. Against this background, the supervisor might then focus on the issue of shift assignments and ask Chernitski to state those conditions under which he might be willing to move to the second shift.

There are other options a mediator can use. A mediator should conduct a caucus in the same purposeful way that she directs other aspects of the discussion. A caucus is not a "rap session." The mediator does not "wing it" in a caucus. She calls for a caucus to gain information or insights that will contribute to developing a settlement. By integrating a selected strategy for generating movement with a developed discussion agenda, she gets the data—and often movement—that will help the situation move forward.

The mediator closes each caucus by asking the party to identify anything they have discussed that the mediator cannot share with the other parties. (Notice the mediator's translation of her original opening remarks regarding confidentiality: the assumption is that the mediator can use anything that is not flagged if it will be useful in developing a resolution.) With the answer in hand, the mediator moves to the next meeting.

The Second Caucus Session

The mediator will always meet in caucus with each of the parties to a dispute before reconvening them in a joint session. She does this to maintain her neutrality. Separate meetings arouse suspicion that private deals are being made, and a mediator who conducts a substantial majority of such sessions with only one party inflames that fear. However, the length of time the mediator spends with all parties need not be identical; the nature and length of these subsequent caucuses is determined by the purpose for which the mediator originally called for the caucus. If, for instance, the mediator declared a caucus in order to confirm movement by one party or to challenge a recalcitrant party to modify its posture, then once she has finished her initial caucus session, her mission is accomplished; there is no substantive need to meet with any of the other parties in separate session. But to preserve her image as impartial, the mediator must extend to each of the other parties the courtesy of meeting alone. She approaches each of them separately and asks whether there is anything the party would like to discuss before she brings everyone together. If the party raises some concerns, the mediator listens and responds accordingly; if the party has nothing new to mention, the mediator invites everyone back into joint session.

However, if the mediator declared the original caucus in order to explore possible settlement options, then she might find herself conducting a series of consecutive caucus sessions with the various parties. When that happens, the challenge is to conduct the sequential sessions in a way that enables her to communicate information, honor confidences, and explore the acceptability of specific settlement terms without disclosing known offers of movement. How does she do that?

Protecting Offers of Movement

A mediator does not conduct caucuses simply to tell one party what the others have said to her privately. The mediator develops her strategy and discussion agenda for subsequent caucuses in the same manner that she follows when conducting the first caucus session. Now, however, she must incorporate into the plan an indirect test for determining whether the terms of agreement that one party has now tentatively accepted are satisfactory to the other.

Using the last example, suppose Chernitski told the supervisor in his initial caucus that he would work a different shift immediately if Chen would pay some amount toward the repair of the damaged tools. The supervisor's job is to find out if that proposed arrangement is acceptable to Chen. How should she proceed?

Suppose the supervisor conducts the caucus with Chen by selecting the fifth strategy listed; that is, she begins by reminding Chen of the cost of not settling. Against that backdrop, she moves to a discussion of the damaged tools and suggests emphatically that there will be no agreement—the costs of not settling will obtain—unless Chen is willing to do something to help Chernitski replace his damaged tools. Chen, if he was assured that the discussion was confidential, might reveal many things to the supervisor: that he damaged the tools because he was fed up with Chernitski's ethnic barbs, that he himself did not damage the tools but that he had prompted his friends to do so, or that he did not damage the tools intentionally but had been drinking beer at lunch (in violation of company rules) and broke them by mistake. Chen might conclude by stating that he is willing to pay Chernitski some money for the repair or replacement of the damaged tools but only on two conditions: that he does not have to admit to Chernitski that he damaged them, and that Chernitski works the second shift.

Eureka! An agreement is at hand. The supervisor now knows that Chernitski and Chen will resolve their dispute as long as the amount of money Chen is willing to pay is acceptable to Chernitski.

Of course, this strategy might not have generated such a welcome response. Or the supervisor might have approached the discussion from a different angle.

But the supervisor would invite disaster if she were to begin her caucus with Chen as follows:

> SUPERVISOR: Chernitski is willing to work the second shift if you pay him something for the damaged tools. Is that acceptable?

Why is this approach a disaster? If the supervisor says this, Chen immediately knows that Chernitski will do what Chen wants him to do—work the second shift; Chen will now try to get Chernitski to do that without giving him anything substantial in return. Thanks to the supervisor's bungling, Chen will have acquired a powerful incentive for digging in his heels and testing whether he can force Chernitski to capitulate.

If, however, a mediator conducts each caucus not by explicitly testing the acceptability of the other's proposals but, rather, by structuring the discussion to learn what specific arrangements each party needs in order to settle, then she will discover whether there is a gap or an overlap in their proposed settlement terms without inadvertently aggravating their tensions.

Protecting the Source

Testing the acceptability of settlement terms in an indirect manner does not mean that a mediator should be coy. Sometimes she needs to find out clearly whether one party will accept specific terms that the mediator knows are acceptable to others. How can she do this without giving away the store? There are two options: she can propose the settlement terms in a hypothetical format, or she can adopt the proposal as her own. Here is how these approaches would work when the supervisor caucuses with Chen:

> SUPERVISOR (Option 1): Let's consider the following possibility. What if Chernitski were to work the second shift and you were to pay him some amount of money toward the repair or replacement of the damaged tools. Would that be an arrangement you could live with?
> SUPERVISOR (Option 2): I don't know if this arrangement would be acceptable but let me toss out the following idea for each of you to consider. Suppose he were to work the second shift and you were to pay him some amount of money toward the repair or replacement of the damaged tools. Could you live with that arrangement?

What are the likely responses to such questions? If Chen finds this an acceptable format, he can respond accordingly. If he tried to accept only part of it ("I'll agree that Chernitski should work the second shift, but I won't pay him any money for the damaged tools"), then the supervisor can either remind Chen that the idea involved two dimensions or force Chen to provide his reasons for such objections (the justification questions) so that she has a better understanding of what it will take to get an agreement. If Chen thinks the entire idea is stupid, he can simply blame the supervisor for it rather than becoming furious at Chernitski for making "one more selfish attempt to squeeze me for the money."

Of course, Chen might respond to the proposed questions by asking sharply: "Did Chernitski tell you he would agree to this?" The supervisor must respond: "I'll have to talk to him about it again, but I won't do that if it is not acceptable to you." Or the supervisor, wanting to communicate a sense of optimism, might hedge her response: "I think I can get him to accept it if you give me something meaningful to work with in terms of compensation for the damaged tools." The supervisor does not lie to Chen by denying that she has discussed this possibility with Chernitski, nor does she become defensive and tell Chen it is none of his business. But she must respond in a way that enables each party to evaluate the proposed settlement terms without knowing whether the terms are acceptable to the other.

By protecting the source of the settlement proposals in either of these two ways, a mediator allows for one other possibility: she preserves for the parties the option of rejecting those terms now but accepting them later in the discussion. A mediator must remember that parties often have only one chance to accept or reject a formally communicated proposal; once a proposal is rejected, it is difficult to revive without at least some modification. Therefore, a mediator must shape her conduct and language in the caucus to be consistent with an informal, but directed, exploration of settlement options.

> *Example 4.* A tenant informs a mediator during a caucus that she is willing to pay $1000 to satisfy all claims for back rent. The mediator, in a caucus with the landlord, floats that possibility as a *hypothetical proposal*; the landlord rejects it. Two hours later the landlord might have a different appreciation of the tenant's problems or a realistic view of what she might be able to get; suddenly, a $1000 settlement may be more attractive and can be revived as a possible settlement option. If, however, the mediator had erred by originally telling the landlord that "the tenant has authorized me to convey to you that she is proposing to pay you $1000 to settle," and the landlord had rejected the proposal, then any subsequent settlement figure might have to be greater than that formal proposal of $1000 (in order for the landlord to "save face," for example—"I already rejected that—I'm not going to accept it now"); that increase, however small it may be, might constitute the difference between a settlement and a stalemate.

Displaying the Agreement

By conducting a caucus, the mediator becomes the first person to know when the parties have reached a settlement. Her task is not over. She must decide how to reveal those terms of agreement to the parties. She has two options: she can have the parties propose them to each other, or she can reveal them and simply ask the parties to confirm their acceptance of them.

By the Parties

There is a decided advantage in having the parties communicate directly to each other what they are willing to do to resolve the dispute. They are the ones who must live with the solution. They must be able to get along with each other at least to the degree called for under their settlement terms. They must feel that the agreement is one they find acceptable rather than one that is being thrust upon them. They begin to rebuild or restore their confidence in each other's commitment to comply with the agreement by hearing the other state explicitly what she is pledging herself to do to resolve the dispute.

If the mediator adopts this approach, she reconvenes the parties following the caucuses and directs them to tell each other what they are prepared to do to resolve the remaining issues in dispute. In the foregoing example, the supervisor would reconvene Chernitski and Chen and say:

> SUPERVISOR: I'd like each of you to tell the other what you discussed with me in our separate sessions regarding how the matters of the damaged tools and shift assignments can be resolved to your satisfaction. Chernitski, why don't you speak first?

The potential disadvantages of proceeding in this way are obvious: the party who speaks might propose terms that differ from those he had accepted during his caucus, or he might preface his statement with such derogatory or self-serving remarks that the other party ends up rejecting terms he had previously indicated were acceptable. It does not matter if the speaker does this deliberately or inadvertently. Either way, the agreement is jeopardized. How can the mediator sidestep that pitfall?

By the Mediator

Sometimes the mediator must tie down the agreement securely; this is particularly true in situations where the mediator senses that the parties are agreeing to do what is necessary to resolve the dispute but remain bitter toward one another or resent some of the settlement terms. To accomplish this, the mediator reconvenes the parties, identifies the unresolved issues, indicates what each party is willing to do or accept to resolve that issue, and asks the parties to confirm her statement. What this approach lacks in fostering communication, it compensates for by being precise and succinct:

> SUPERVISOR: With regard to the matter of the shift assignment, Chernitski agrees to work the second shift beginning next week and Chen will remain on the first shift. Is that right?

Whether we are trying to prevent acts of violence at a protest, resolve a contract dispute, reduce the possibility of the outbreak of gang wars, assist neighborhood residents in working out differences with government agencies over planned development, or help our children solve disagreements between them, we often choose to talk with each party alone and then with everyone together. Caucusing can be very useful. It generates a sense of confidence and intimacy between the party and the mediator. It invites candor and encourages an un-inhibited exploration of solutions.

Caucusing has drawbacks though. It takes time. It transfers the responsibility for communication from the parties to the mediator; it introduces the possibility that the mediator inaccurately communicates what is said, further inflaming the dispute. It impedes the development of creative energy that flows from a lively exchange and interaction among discussants. And it robs the parties of a chance to build a collaborative negotiation relationship with one another—particularly important for parties with ongoing relationships.

So a mediator must use caucusing selectively. She must not hesitate to use it when appropriate, but she must realize that she does not need to use it in every dispute.

11

Reach Closure

There's no problem, only solutions.

John Lennon

All mediated discussions must eventually end. When they do, the parties should have a clearer understanding of their situation and, in many cases, an agreement that promotes their interests. Sometimes no mutually acceptable resolution emerges from the mediation; the parties, however, may be better positioned to develop a resolution at a later time or to move on to some other dispute resolution process. This chapter examines the different outcomes that are possible: agreement—on substance or process—and no agreement. Where resolutions are reached, the mediator wants the agreement—whether it is written or oral—to be as doable and durable as possible to prevent future disputes. An agreement that is both appealing and clear, in addition to being interest satisfying for each party, is most likely to be successful.

Whatever the outcome, the mediator plays an active role in staging the final act. He wants the close of the session to be as constructive as possible. He wants to minimize harm and maximize benefit from the mediation.

Outcomes

Whatever parties decide to do, the mediator will want their decision to be informed by an enriched understanding and tempered by a realistic assessment of their situation. If a party rashly agrees to pay $50,000 tomorrow to settle a claim, the mediator will want to inquire whether (and how) this can be done. If a party decides to walk away without an agreement, the mediator will want him to have thought through what he is walking towards. In other words, the parties should thoughtfully embrace the chosen outcome. Parties can choose to agree or not to agree; the mediator should ensure that decisions are well considered at least and, at best, as optimal as possible to meet the parties' interests.

Agreement

A primary goal of mediated discussions is to have disputing parties resolve substantive issues in a mutually acceptable way. When all issues are resolved, closure is complete. What happens, though, when parties agree to resolve less than all issues?

If the mediator helps the parties resolve some but not all of the substantive issues, then the parties can: (1) agree on a process for handling the unresolved issues, or (2) agree to implement those matters on which they have agreed even though other matters remain unsettled. If the mediator can get the parties to agree on a process for handling the unresolved substantive issues (for example, sending a matter to a committee for study), then the parties, in fact, will have resolved all outstanding matters; they will have a complete agreement. But what if that move does not succeed?

In some contexts, such as when a union and management are negotiating terms of a new collective bargaining agreement, the parties adopt a procedural framework that makes final agreement on any one issue contingent on resolution of all matters; everything is "tentatively agreed to" until all elements of the package are adopted. If, for example, parties agree on an expanded vacation schedule, increased health benefits, and less cumbersome work rules, but cannot agree on new wage rates, then they have no agreement on any issue. Obviously, a mediator tries to persuade the parties to reach agreement on wages so they do not lose the benefits they have provisionally secured. He does this by pointing out to them the costs of not settling. Under this procedural framework, however, if an agreement on wages is not reached, then no agreements stand.

Unless the parties have agreed in advance to such an all-or-nothing governing procedure, then whether parties implement those substantive matters that they have resolved, even though other issues remain unresolved, depends on two factors: (1) the substantive interrelationship between the resolved and unresolved issues, and (2) the comparative importance of the resolved and unresolved issues.

1. *Issue independence or dependence.* Suppose two salespersons argue heatedly with their supervisor over which one is entitled to the commission for a

previous sale. The supervisor (mediator) can get them to implement their agreement not to make sarcastic remarks or berate one another during their forthcoming joint presentation to a new client, even though the compensation issue remains unresolved; the two matters are related but independent of one another. However, if the corporate president gets his division leaders to agree to decentralize the company's personnel function among its twenty retail stores but fails to have them agree on a timetable for doing so, then, absent a direct order on the matter of timing, no one can implement that decentralization agreement because of the dependence of the resolved issue on the unresolved issue.

2. *Priority of issue.* Parties can reach agreement on issues that can be implemented independently of each other, but if the resolved issue is trivial and the unresolved matter important, then the parties have no incentive to implement their agreement. Suppose a government agency suddenly changes its program priorities and, as a result, immediately terminates its funding of those private agencies that no longer administer high-priority projects and reallocates their former budgets to those persons involved with high-priority endeavors. Four weeks later, after the directors of the affected projects had protested the action, the government agency agrees to provide six-months notice of program budget cuts to any agency whose funding was cut but refuses to have that policy apply retroactively. That commitment for future action is of almost no value to the agencies that had lost their current funding and might have already terminated some staff members or closed business operations. Thus, although it is accurate to state that the disputants have agreed on some matters that could be implemented, the value of their implementation is sharply reduced when considered in light of those issues that remain unresolved.

Even if the mediator does not succeed in helping the parties reach agreement on the substantive issues in dispute, he tries to have them agree on a process for resolving them. When mediated discussions collapse, the most destabilizing factor is that one party can now act unilaterally and without notice. Such actions invariably alter the *status quo* and force the other party to escalate to protect their interests. For example, where parties to a divorce proceeding fail to agree on separation terms, one spouse might secretly take the children out of the jurisdiction before a judicial decree is rendered. To avoid damaging escalation, the mediator may be able to get parties to agree to maintain the *status quo* for a specified period, try some new arrangement for a "trial period," obtain counseling, resolve the matters in court or arbitration, seek legislative reform, or do nothing for a "cooling off" period. The value of such an agreement is that it establishes reliable expectations on which to base short-term plans.

No Agreement

Some mediated discussions end without any resolution of the negotiating issues. No mediator should try to camouflage that fact. But he must try to make certain the parties leave the discussions without feeling any more bitterness toward one another than they did before the meeting and with a clearer idea of their options.

The mediator does not want the parties to leave feeling incapable of dealing with their situation. He can discharge his duty as scapegoat at this juncture by expressing to all parties his regret that he was unable to help them resolve their dispute. Even if the mediator believes that the parties are unreasonable, he does not tell them so, but attributes their lack of success to his own inability to help them. This does not fool anyone, but it does allow the parties to leave the discussion without undue anger or despair.

The mediator also highlights what the parties have accomplished during their talks. The absence of a settlement does not mean the discussions were useless. The mediated discussion may well have clarified issues more precisely, developed a more credible information base, canvassed the strengths and weaknesses of the parties' litigation positions, explored various settlement options, and improved communication among the parties by piercing inflammatory rhetoric. These are not insignificant elements of progress; although the mediator must not exaggerate their value, he should bring them to the parties' attention so that they do not leave the meeting in utter frustration.

Forms of Agreement

Mediated agreements are either written or oral. Most terms of agreement are explicit, but some are deliberately vague. Some identify specific behavioral elements that parties agree to perform; others describe more general aspirations.

Whatever form the agreement takes, the mediator must make certain people understand what it is that they are agreeing to. If co-workers have resolved their dispute over who gets the corner office with the window, the mediator must make that explicit; if they have agreed to postpone a decision on that matter for three weeks, he must make that clear.

Written Agreements

A variety of written formats capture terms of agreement: a signed contract stating what each party promises to do, a memorandum of understanding between the parties, a jointly-issued press release, a letter from the mediator to the parties identifying what everyone has agreed to, written proposals exchanged between the parties and initialed by the negotiators and the mediator to reflect agreement on the various matters, and a straightforward change in the written statement of a particular policy, law, or practice that incorporates the terms of agreement.

There are obvious benefits to a written agreement. Writing makes the terms of agreement explicit and thus prevents disputes about what parties agreed to do. It gives parties a chance to review their commitments before officially "signing off" on them. It prevents parties from adding or deleting obligations. It serves as a future reference for checking compliance. Finally, and not insignificantly, it represents to the parties the one tangible, concrete piece of evidence of their mutual success.

Writing agreements is an art and a science. The mediator may be the scribe of the agreement—or at least a draft of the agreement. Or, the mediator may coach the parties or their attorneys in writing the agreement. Practices vary with respect to who holds the pen (or controls the keyboard). In any case, though, the mediator will want to help the parties craft a document that is both appealing and clear.

Appealing

The parties must want to sign the agreement. Here are some guidelines for making an agreement appealing.

1. *Names.* Parties care that their proper names appear and are correct. They will be offended by the use of a nickname or their name's misspelling in an important document. Names are powerful, and the mediator should use them, avoiding legal jargon like "party of the first part" or "plaintiff."

2. *Order of provisions.* A major component of the mediator's job is developing a logical order for discussing issues. The order in which agreement terms are listed is also important. To make an agreement more appealing for everyone: begin with a statement of common interests and goals; then start with those

commitments that entail a mutual obligation to act ("Smith and Jones agree not to make sarcastic remarks about each other during their joint presentation to new customers"); finally, place less burdensome commitments first ("Jones agrees to email Smith about any new appointments the same day the appointment is made"). Just as discussions can profit from positive momentum and investment in successes, so can the adoption of and commitment to an agreement.

3. *Balance.* A mediator must not list twenty items that party A agrees to do for party B and then the five items that party B agrees to do for party A. Disperse them so that one party does not feel outmatched by the other, or rewrite them so the twenty items are reduced to five categories. Similarly, a mediator should not reference one party as "Professor Smith" and the other as "Jane."

4. *Format.* The format of the agreement should enable people easily to find what their obligations are. This takes some imagination. Use headings; the issues (listed in the mediator's notes in the "A" and "D" of BADGER) will provide the headings for the agreement. Use numbers and letters to mark each undertaking and any sub-part of that undertaking. If there are charts and graphs that detail the specific terms of agreement, summarize them in the body of the agreement and attach them as an appendix. If the agreement is long, develop a table of contents for it.

5. *General appearance.* Writing the agreement in pencil on the back of an envelope might produce a chuckle from U.S. history students, but it undermines the importance that most people attach to the resolution of their dispute. If possible, an agreement should be clean, neat, and attractive.

6. *Admissions of wrongdoing.* A party may or may not admit wrongdoing as the basis for agreeing to perform in a certain way. But such admissions have no place in a written agreement. A mediator must adopt nonjudgmental language:

> NOT: Inga Stanek agrees to pay Xavier Griffin $550.00 in full payment for the bicycle that she stole from Griffin's son, Joe, on November 1.

> BUT: Inga Stanek agrees to pay Xavier Griffin $550.00 in full payment for the replacement of Joe Griffin's bicycle that disappeared on November 1.

7. *Tone.* The agreement must state clearly what each party agrees to do without lengthy explanations or accusations.

> DON'T WRITE: Ellis agrees that his loud playing of the sound system after 11:00 p.m. on Sunday through Thursday nights is rude and in-

considerate of Korman's rights and therefore agrees to wear earphones whenever he plays his sound system after 11:00 p.m. on those nights.

WRITE: Ellis agrees to wear earphones whenever he plays his sound system after 11:00 p.m. on Sunday through Thursday nights.

8. *Omissions or additions.* The mediator should write down everything that the parties have agreed to do, and no more. The mediator invites lasting hostility if, in the writing process, he mistakenly adds to or subtracts from the parties' verbal commitments.

Clear

The agreement must be understandable to the parties. They are the ones that will do what is written. It must give sufficient guidance to avoid misunderstanding and further disputes. The agreement should use language that precisely captures what the parties undertake. Ambiguities must be uncovered and deliberate ambiguities must be clearly stated. Here are the most common traps to avoid:

1. *Parties' own words.* Even if the parties use language that is less elegant or sophisticated than what the mediator might write, their own words will be more meaningful and more powerful than anyone else's. The agreement should reflect the words that the parties use and speak in a language the parties understand. If divorcing parents want their child to have a "carefree" and "joyful" childhood, the legal standard of "best interests of the child" should not be substituted for their words. Teenagers agreeing not to "dis" each other should not find that translated to an agreement to be "cordial to one another."

2. *Plain English.* Just because an agreement might be a binding legal document, it does not mean it should be full of long and undecipherable words. "Heretofore" and "aforesaid" will never make an agreement more durable.

3. *Pronouns.* Pronouns invite ambiguity, so minimize their use. Here is an excerpt from one agreement:

> If Ms. T believes that Ms. K has not complied with the terms of this agreement, she will contact her through her attorney.

Is Ms. T to contact Ms. K by having Ms. T's attorney contact Ms. K., or is Ms. T supposed to contact Ms. K's attorney, who will relay the message to Ms. K? An agreement should not be an obstacle course. Make it clear.

SAMPLE AGREEMENT PROVISIONS

> **LEGEND:**
> Common interests→**Bold**
> Issues→SMALL CAPS
> Proposals that are mutually acceptable→*Italics*

Employer and Employee want to end their employment relationship in an amicable manner. To that end, they agree:

1. EMPLOYMENT RELATIONSHIP.
   A. EMPLOYEE'S EMPLOYMENT STATUS. **Both Employer and Employee would like to facilitate Employee's smooth transition to a new job.** Consequently, they agree:
      i. *that Employee shall remain at the company for three months with full pay and benefits, retaining his current office, telephone and e-mail privileges, and job title. During that period Employee shall look for other employment and shall have no job-related responsibilities. At the end of that period, Employee shall resign; and*
      ii. *that Employer shall provide Employee with out placement services at a provider chosen by Employee for one year or until Employee is hired (whichever occurs sooner).*
   B. CLAIMS AGAINST EMPLOYER. **Both Employer and Employee want no further disputes.** Consequently, they agree:
      i. *that Employee will sign a release...*

---

4. *Abbreviations.* Even the most innocent of abbreviations can generate conflicting interpretations. If a tenant agrees on October 10, 2012, to vacate his apartment on 1/10/13, the landlord might think that his tenant will leave on January 10, 2013, and the tenant may believe he can stay until October 1, 2013. Since the written agreement will take precedence over any verbal understandings, a party might exploit this careless use of abbreviations to its maximum advantage.

5. *Methods of performance.* Some terms of agreement can be executed in more than one way. A mediator must persuade parties to perform their obligations in a manner that can be verified and is most likely to achieve full compliance. If one party agrees to return items by mail, the mediator might clarify whether FedEx or U.S. mail-return receipt requested would best ensure timely and verifiable compliance. The agreement should accurately reflect the address to which the items should be mailed. Similarly, the mediator must write the agreement so that parties do not pay their debts with personal checks that can be dribbled to the bank!

6. *Timing of performance.* If parties agree to do something for one another, it is critical to pin down WHEN. If the payee expects that a payment will be made tomorrow and the payor believes that the payment can be made "sometime soon," those differing expectations can cause a new dispute.

7. *Evaluative terms.* What does it mean when someone promises to divide the toy trucks among the children "fairly," to repair the roof "satisfactorily," or to act "reasonably" or "in good faith"? These terms and phrases are meaningful concepts, but they are elastic in nature and do not identify explicitly those standards of performance against which one can evaluate compliance. A mediator must use such terms deliberately. If the parties agree that a "fair" division of toy trucks requires that every child have at least one toy, then the mediator must say so; if the roof repair is measured according to the subjective standard of being satisfactory to the owner rather than the more objective criterion of "meeting industry standards," he must make that explicit.

The mediator cannot make the mistake of believing that his job is done when the parties have verbally agreed to a resolution of the issues. He is needed— either as a scribe or coach—for the drafting process. The agreement is a photograph of what the parties have agreed to do. If it is appealing and clear, it is far more likely that it will also be durable.

Verbal Agreements

In some contexts it is unnecessary or inappropriate to write down what the disputants have agreed to do. A person acting as a go-between among coworkers who are arguing over who should clean up the mess left in the photocopying room does not commit their agreement to writing—people just do what they have agreed to do. The same principle applies when a parent helps his children resolve a confrontation or a teacher resolves a dispute between two students who are fighting in the classroom.

Some disputes are resolved with a handshake; others conclude with an apology or a promise to behave in a certain manner in the future. Such informal resolutions do not mean that the disputes or their solutions are insignificant. A mediator cannot get caught in the trap of believing that important matters must be resolved in a written format while unimportant issues can be resolved otherwise.

Consider a typical employment situation in which one supervisor is uniformly despised by his subordinates because he uses offensive language, favors one employee when granting overtime work assignments, and disciplines some but not all employees for arriving late to work. During contract negotiations, the union proposes a series of demands that would stop these practices; because of the nature of collective bargaining, however, the union must propose rules that apply to all supervisors. An employer might acknowledge the legitimacy of the employees' concerns regarding the one supervisor but have reservations about adopting the proposed rules on a company-wide basis. The resolution? The employer makes a verbal commitment to the union to discipline and reassign the supervisor in exchange for the union withdrawing its proposal on this matter. No employer or union would commit such an agreement to writing, for the employer wants to handle the discipline of its supervisor privately and on job-related grounds that are consistent with company and legal practices. But the employer is as much obliged, practically speaking, to do what he has orally agreed to do as he would be if he had reduced the commitment to writing, for failure to comply might result in the employees engaging in a job slowdown or wildcat strike.

Not putting things in writing permits people to comply with the terms of agreement while continuing to rant and rave. A mediator might be able to get the owner of a local television station and a civil rights organization to agree to a general plan for hiring more minority personnel in key corporate positions. Not committing that agreement to writing, however, enables the owner to condemn publicly quota hiring systems while he quietly acts according to the agreed-on affirmative action hiring program that, in content, bears a striking resemblance to the very systems he criticizes.

While a mediator cannot be lulled into the false belief that oral commitments are less important than written ones, he must remember that actions speak louder than words; in the end, what people do to resolve their dispute is far more important than either what they say they will do to resolve it or what they pledge in writing to do. That observation is not meant to minimize the importance of written agreements nor to suggest that oral commitments are useless; rather, it is meant to put their value in some perspective. Ultimately, substance triumphs over form. At some point, people do what they are obliged to do not because they said or wrote that they would. Rather, they continue to honor their commitments, and the spirit of their commitments, because they conclude that their counterparts will do likewise. On the basis of the other party's performance, an individual or group develops confidence that others will not deliberately undercut their aspirations or interests. Reciprocity of conduct takes hold. Soon, each party does not need to check their agreement every time he acts. Relationships are too rich to be bound by such an artificial straitjacket.

Closure to the Session

When discussions end, whether or not an agreement has been reached, the parties are likely to have strong feelings. In some cases, parties may feel satisfied and uplifted. In other cases, they may feel burdened and hopeless. The mediator's job is to make sure that they do not leave feeling worse than when they came and that they feel as positive as they can under the circumstances. How can the mediator close the session to be sure that it is as constructive as possible?

Just like an opening statement, the mediator's closing remarks should target certain topics.

1. *Status of discussions.* The mediator plays a critical role in keeping track of progress on every issue. Each mediation session should end with a summary of where things stand. If there is an agreement, each element of the agreement should be reviewed and the agreement should be signed. If there is no agreement on some or all issues, options for further action should be summarized.

2. *Mediator responsibility for less than full resolution.* If the parties completely resolve their dispute, they should be congratulated. If, however, some or all of the issues are unresolved, the mediator should lighten the burden of that perceived failure by playing the scapegoat. "I'm sorry I was unable to help you resolve all the issues you raised today." Such a statement takes some of the load off the parties and raises the possibility that another approach on another day might be more fruitful.

3. *Acknowledgment of parties' negotiation skills.* The mediator is an educator. Pointing out to the parties what they did well not only will make them feel good, but also will highlight attitudes and moves that they should display in future negotiations. "Thank you both for agreeing to mediate and

staying with it for four hours today. Your willingness to try, plus patience and perseverance, were what it took to resolve this." "You did a good job of listening to one another and coming up with options. Those same skills will be helpful in finding some resolution going forward." Whatever is said must be true and sincere. By listing out the parties' accomplishments, the mediator makes it more likely that they will do those helpful things in the future.

4. *Recognition of the difficulty of the situation.* It is not easy to be in a dispute and come to mediation. The simple recognition of the challenge makes parties feel comforted about the difficulty and heartened by their own strength. The mediator says simply: "I recognize it was not easy for you to come today or to stay as long as you did. It was a privilege to help you. Good job."

5. *Optimism for eventual resolution or the success of the agreement.* The mediator should be a spring of energy and momentum. Encouraging the parties to press on in terms of seeking new options (if there was no agreement) or abiding by their agreement (if there was one) is important. "While we didn't reach a resolution today, I trust that new ideas will emerge as time goes by." "You have reached agreement that resolves your dispute; now turn your focus towards making the agreement work." "Given the effort you made today, it seems likely you will find success."

6. *Invitation to return.* Many mediators are in a business. Some are acting as volunteers. In either case, the mediator wants parties to leave feeling the door is open if they want to try mediation again. The mediator says, "If at any point you feel it would be helpful to use mediation again, I (or a particular mediation program or firm) would be delighted to assist you."

At that point the mediator announces the close of the session. He wants to make sure that parties leave the session at the same time. Often, someone wants to linger to review the process or outcome with the mediator. That is a bad idea because the departing party may feel a lack of impartiality—the final words are being spoken with no opportunity for him to take part. So the mediator—with a handshake and goodbye—indicates that the mediation is finished. In some cases, where tensions have been high, the mediator might also want to discuss arrangements for parties to leave separately so they do not find themselves in a small elevator with a renewed opportunity for tension.

In the days to come, parties must place their dispute and its resolution in perspective. They must determine the priority they will continue to attach to it as they conduct their daily routine. They must deal with both its resolution and the consequences of the way in which they tried to resolve it.

The mediator's efforts and contributions to the process are evaluated independently of the particular resolution the parties reach. A mediator has not failed if the parties do not successfully resolve all their negotiating issues. Rather he should measure his success by the energy, diligence and skill he has displayed in each part of the BADGER process.

Part 4

The Lessons of Experience

12

Embracing Diversity Dynamics

What we have to do . . . is find a way to celebrate our diversity and debate our differences without fracturing our communities.

Hillary Rodham Clinton

BADGER was presented as though it made no difference whether the mediator or individual parties are a man or woman; young or old; rich or poor; Caucasian, African American or Hispanic; raised in a Western or Eastern culture; or followers of a particular religion or atheists.

But this cannot be the entire story. Differences matter. Why? Because some differences generate the conduct that creates the conflict and the issues that a mediator is committed to helping resolve.

The question is not whether differences exist—of course they do. The important questions are: Which differences count in a mediation, and why? Eye color? Height? Age? Sibling order? Hometown? Religious beliefs? Conversational pace? Work experience? Educational training? Being left handed?

Questions about diversity raise concerns about values and practices. Not all are relevant to the mediator, so she must decide which warrant her attention and which do not. She must know what standards, principles or considerations are appropriate for making that judgment. And she must then incorporate that understanding into BADGER in a way that helps her look for, understand, and embrace these differences to conduct a constructive conversation. That is a challenging task.

The Context of "Culture"

It is not possible to catalogue every difference that might impact how people interact with each other and with the mediator. The following elements, though, represent the basic architecture of differences that do matter to a mediator. They are described below within the general framework of an understanding of "culture."

A culture is a group of persons that has a common set of beliefs, customs and convictions. The group often has a distinctive language and set of symbols.

When one thinks of cultural differences among persons, one tends to envision people from different countries, believing, for example, that people from the United States reflect a different culture than that of people from Brazil, Italy or China. That perspective is not false, but it is dangerously misleading for a mediator.

A culture is not defined simply by geographical boundaries of a contemporary nation-state. There are many groups with distinctive cultures, wherever those persons might reside; for example, whether persons live in England, Spain, Argentina, or the United States, there is a culture among the group (formal or not) of persons who are lawyers or engineers or doctors or teachers or musicians or artists; among management and labor; among mothers of school-age children; in the U.S., among southerners and northerners; among Christians, Jews and Muslims; among political conservatives, moderates, and liberals. And the list goes on.

What is the significance of noting that culture is not defined geographically?

A given group—culture—and its members engage in distinctive practices, wherever those persons live. And those practices might lead to misunderstandings and conflict.

For example, an Asian-Indian male who is a U.S. citizen and lives in an apartment building in Chicago, Illinois might cook spicy foods with rich aromas that are part of his Asian-Indian culture; but when those aromas fill the hallway, his non-Indian neighbors might complain because they are unfamiliar with, or annoyed by, the smell. Producers of a television show in Great Britain might present a program that mocks or satirizes the practices of a particular religious group, and, in so doing, offend other community members who are members of that religion. Or a person at the worksite who is vegan might be systematically excluded from participating in staff luncheon events because the menu options consist entirely of meat dishes. So there can be cultural clashes within one's own geographic community.

This point warrants repeated emphasis. Cultural diversity dynamics occur in almost every mediation session, whether the conflict involves neighbors in an Atlanta, Georgia suburb, unions and management at a New York City hospital, businesspersons from Dallas and St. Louis, or policy makers from Oregon and Wyoming. A mediator does not need mediation parties who live in different countries—Spain and Germany or Brazil and the Unites States—before she must pay attention to diversity considerations.

Two important insights emerge from these observations: first, one person can be a part of many cultures. Second, despite differences among persons of different cultures, persons of different cultures also share similarities, and a mediator wants that to be the case because she can help parties build mutually acceptable outcomes on the basis of both the differences and the similarities. Parties who are Muslim and Hindi, for example, may clash in that respect, but, if the parties are both women with children they may have much in common.

What Differences Matter?

The fundamental question about diversity can be restated in an enriched way: what differences—and what similarities—among the participants ought to matter to the mediator?

The required subjects fall into one of two categories: Customs and Convictions.

Customs

A group can have many customs: a distinctive handshake; a ceremonial graduation exercise; a special meal for a particular event or holiday. No mediator can know all customs for all groups. What should she focus on? *Target those that shape or influence the manner in which a person or group conducts a negotiation.*

Communication Styles

As stated in Chapter 7, people communicate verbally and non-verbally, and a mediator must support both forms. But the communication patterns and practices of a given group may be distinctive. How?

1. *Formality.* Some cultures and individuals are more formal than others.

If someone is called "Jake" who expected to be called Dr. Smith, he might be deeply offended. If an email does not contain a respectful salutation "Dear Csilla" and a closure "With Warm Regards", it might receive a cold reception. If an emoticon, like :), is used with a highly formal person, it might result in disdain. When communicating orally, those cultures that are more formal might expect an individual to stand when making her comments, while less formal approaches endorse communicating while seated.

Many novice mediators believe that since "mediation is an informal process," all their communications with participants should be informal. Bad mistake. A mediator must learn the communication style of her participants. The mediator's safest practice, always, is to start formally—she can move towards informality if the situation warrants.

2. *Clarity.* Persons in some cultures expect that much is understood from the context and need not be said. For instance, Hisako (from Japan) might say "yes" and it is understood to other Japanese present, given the context, that she means "no"; people in Turkey might say "no" when offered food, knowing from the context that it must be offered three times to be a real offer. By contrast, persons in other cultures "say what they mean and mean what they say." If mediation parties differ on this dimension, then a mediator must adjust, making certain, for example, not to unfairly press more vigorously for movement from the party whose communication style is contextually based by misinterpreting that party's negotiating conduct as being vague or indecisive.

3. *Intensity.* In some cultures, being highly emotional and loudly expressing views is expected and even desirable because it shows involvement. Many family conversations exhibit this strong, animated communication style. In other cultures, "polite discourse" means communicating verbally in a calm manner, letting each speaker complete her comments before responding, not showing anger or using coarse language, and the like. Many mediators prefer that disputants engage in a deliberate, reasonably quiet conversation. That is understandable, but dangerous. If a mediator completely shuts down one communication style because it is upsetting or uncomfortable to the other party or to the mediator, she may have instantly compromised her being perceived as neutral. More important, she may have eliminated one crucial avenue for gaining information about how strongly a participant feels about a particular matter and what that person's priorities might be. A mediator must work collaboratively with the participants to find space for different communication styles.

4. *Certainty.* Some cultures prefer that every aspect of a deal be spelled out. Others are more comfortable with ambiguity. Lawyers, for instance, to avoid uncertainty for clients may want to address and resolve as many possible con-

tingencies as they can envision and then insist that those provisions be included in a detailed, often lengthy, written contract. In other cultures—many businesspersons, for instance—principals are comfortable with a handshake or an "oral understanding in principle." If these different cultures are present in a mediation session and they collide, one side might believe that a deal has been reached, the other does not, and each begins to lose patience, become frustrated, and edge towards accusing the other of behaving in bad faith. A mediator must skillfully weave this conversation so that parties do not lose sight of both the progress and agreements that they may have, in fact, achieved and the precise points of their remaining disagreements.

Habits and Practices

1. *Time.* People value punctuality differently. Those who value it highly may conclude that persons who come late to a meeting are irresponsible, rude or selfish, while those from cultures that attach lower priority to punctuality, at least for some occasions, may warmly embrace people who arrive after the announced start time. Divorce mediators report that differences in understanding lateness is usual in marital disputes; one partner appears regularly 10 minutes after the appointed meeting time and feels she is on time, and the other partner feels that this lateness shows remarkable disrespect.

Because these differing cultural values regarding punctuality can trigger misunderstandings and conflicts, a mediator must attend to them. If one group predictably treats the announced start time of the mediation as flexible, a mediator must make a special effort to ensure either that the start time is honored or that a more relaxed compliance is expected by—and acceptable to—all participants. Sponsoring a coffee hour as parties convene is one way to soften, if not camouflage, there being a sharp beginning point.

2. *Space.* What is a comfortable spatial distance between people? The answer differs among cultures and individuals, and those differences may generate discomfort or conflict. If someone is experienced as being too close physically, the proximity may result in an accusation that she is "in my face". Such unwanted closeness can feel like an attempt to coerce. By contrast, if the distance is experienced as being too far away, that person may feel disconnected or isolated. A mediator, when establishing the physical arrangements of the meeting facility, must pay attention to such matters as the size of the table (if any) and the distances between both the mediator and each party as well as between the parties; from that starting point, she must monitor and interpret accurately any physical movement by one party towards the other or towards the

mediator. The mediator must be constantly attuned to this dynamic to insure party comfort and engagement.

3. *Eye Contact.* In some cultures, direct and sustained eye contact is a sign of sincerity, truth telling, and confidence; "look me in the eye when you are talking to me" or "I know that he is telling a lie because he could not look me in the face when he described what happened" are typical expressions in many U.S. settings. By contrast, in some cultures in other parts of the world, making direct eye contact, for example, with someone of the opposite gender or someone who is a social superior is disrespectful and can be interpreted as an aggressive, offensive act; if such a participant were to perceive a conventional U.S. mediator as an authority figure and so did not look at her while communicating, that mediator might make a serious mistake if she were to interpret that lack of eye contact as indicia of lying.

4. *Food.* "Breaking bread together" or sharing a meal or snack allows parties to enjoy an activity together and meet a common human need for sustenance; when negotiating parties eat together, the possibility exists that some trust-building communications between them might occur. On the other hand, practices relating to food and eating can generate tensions.

In some cultures, hosts invite their foreign business negotiators to participate together in a meal before any conversation about business transactions occurs; the meal is related to the negotiation even though business is not discussed. In other settings, host negotiators provide food and meals to support negotiators being able to perform their tasks but do not schedule those events in a way that delays or undermines their engaging in business dialogue. If one party views the host's proposed dinner as a stalling tactic or power grab, rather than as a graceful social event, it might undermine the talks from the beginning.

Similarly, if a mediator provides food or refreshments to participants in order to put persons at ease and create a constructive comfort zone, she will undermine her goals if she fails to remember the differing food customs of the participants: some persons, for instance, might not eat meat (vegetarians) and others might eat food but only if prepared in a certain manner (kosher food for people of the Jewish faith). Being a good host requires being sensitive to those needs. And if a mediator does not know the parties' food practices, it is easy to learn: one simply asks: "is there any type of food (refreshment? drink?) that you are not able to consume?" People appreciate the courtesy.

5. *Negotiating contexts and styles.* People presume and expect that engaging in a negotiation about a particular transaction is appropriate in some settings but not in others; and when they negotiate, they do so with different expecta-

tions and approaches.

The conventional wisdom is that in certain contexts—for example, an outdoor bazaar in Istanbul, Turkey or an arts festival in Santa Fe, New Mexico—a customer and merchant expect and delight in engaging in a lengthy negotiation dance with each other about the purchase price of a rug or an art object. If one tries to short-circuit the dance and quickly "seal the deal," one party may be unhappy because the conduct rejects the social ritual of bargaining.

In sharp contrast, we often assume that when purchasing an airline ticket or fulfilling the required number of credit hours to earn a college degree, there is no room to negotiate: either one pays the public price of that provider or complies with the published University rules regarding minimum hours for graduation, or one pursues her best alternative.

So context matters, and the mediator must be attuned to the operative setting. The dominant culture—and indeed other cultural influences—in each setting will result in negotiators using particular styles and tactics.

For instance, when negotiating to buy a product in a market bazaar, the parties' conduct is often described as an example of competitive bargaining: each party starts with a high or low proposal, expecting the other side to know that there is room for a counterproposal; then, following an exchange of continually adjusted proposals that reflect a compromise from their previous proposals, the parties ultimately strike a deal.

Others negotiate by simply trying to assert their power: they try to coerce, intimidate, or otherwise motivate someone to buy an item or perform an action. The person who suddenly appears and offers to check the car engine for the tourist who is filling her car tank with gas and then proposes that the tourist pay for his services effectively develops a negotiated transaction, even if the event is disconcerting or frightening to the tourist. While that process might more accurately be described as someone imposing a deal, sometimes an acceptable exchange is achieved.

And still other persons approach the negotiation with an explicit attempt to explore possibilities with joint sharing of information, collaborative brainstorming events, and an acknowledgement that the proposed outcome must be acceptable not only to the negotiating counterparts but to the larger community of which they are a part.

While such styles—competitive, domineering and collaborative—differ importantly, diversity differences can penetrate even more deeply. Some persons focus on addressing one matter at a time in a linear sequence, while others are more comfortable considering many matters at once. A mediator who fails to appreciate these different decision-making orientations might unwittingly disempower one participant.

Further, does one's gender incline one to prefer conducting a dialogue in a particular way? There is evidence that women interrupt an oral conversation more frequently than do men but that the nature of their interruption is supportive and collaborative, not competitive. If that is so, then does a mediator's ground rule that "only one person speak at a time" unwittingly favor the male participant? The mediator must watch to see whether dialogue is flourishing for all parties.

6. *Hierarchies.* Hierarchical structures within and among groups differ across cultures. In some settings, hierarchies exist but access to each level is open to all; in other settings, access may be restricted by gender, birth order, or religious commitment. Hierarchical relationships impact who speaks; who has authority to make or accept bargaining proposals; and the desirability of each party's best alternative to a negotiated agreement. The mediator must be attentive to these dimensions.

Hierarchical relationships can also reflect and sustain power differences. Professor-student or supervisor-subordinate relationships are easy examples. Others are more indirect and subtle, as when one spouse to a marriage seeks to use his economic capacity to establish his authority over family finances or the educational or religious training of children. As noted previously, no mediator ever presumes that one party has all the power and that the other is completely powerless, but no mediator can or should ignore these power differentials and how they shape bargaining conduct and possible outcomes.

The mediator's continuing challenge is to weave conversations in such a way that respects the presumptive hierarchical structures but is not paralyzed by them.

Convictions

Norms are standards that are used to guide or evaluate conduct. They exist in all settings, including business communities, professional groups, and families. People appeal to them not to explain behavior but rather, more importantly, to evaluate, criticize or commend conduct. "You ought to keep your promise" is a moral norm, as is "do not intentionally inflict pain upon innocent children." Examples of norms in the economic context include "Conduct your business so as to maximize profits" or "Do not maximize business profits at the expense of contaminating the air."

Norms vary in importance. They can often conflict, both within and between contexts. They can be debatable and contentious. Ultimately, they must be justified, not simply asserted. But, like news stories, we often focus on norms that conflict or create tension, overlooking the important fact that people embrace and live by shared norms: "treat people with courtesy and respect" is widely practiced, as is "tell the truth."

So the mediator's wants to pay attention to what norms are in play and how they might dovetail. How does this play out in practice?

Cultures, political traditions, and religious practices embrace many norms that can influence people's conduct and generate conflicts. For example, in some religions, people observe a Sabbath day by refraining from using any item or object that requires non-natural power sources, such as electricity; the practices of other religions on this point permit their use. If persons of these different religions live in the same publicly financed high-rise apartment building and they are trying to develop an acceptable policy regarding the assignment of vacant apartments to current or future residents, how, if at all, should these differing norms be addressed? Should the 70-year old practicing Orthodox Jew who will not use an elevator on her Sabbath day be given preference for an apartment location on one of the lower floors so that she can comfortably walk the stairways to her apartment when going to and from the synagogue to celebrate the Sabbath? Or consider the Department of Chemistry in a public university determining when to schedule one of its basic courses that all students must take if they wish to take advanced training in chemistry; must the Department schedule the course so that students whose religion calls for a daily prayer session at a prescribed hour are not systematically excluded from enrolling in it? At a minimum, relevant norms must be thoughtfully considered.

Further, there are many deep, explosive controversies fueled by differing norms regarding child rearing and autonomy. Should the parents of a 7-year old daughter, pursuant to their religious beliefs, be able to hire a medical doctor to perform female genital mutilation on their daughter at a public hospital in the United States or should that hospital have the right to prohibit that procedure?

Even when differing, and perhaps conflicting, group norms do not constitute the focus of the dispute, they may impact how parties participate in a mediated negotiation. A simple, but important, example is how different cultures treat physical contact—touching—among persons. In certain faith communities, men cannot touch women unrelated by marriage or blood. Some cultures view a "soft" handshake as meek rather than polite, a "firm" handshake as respectful rather than overpowering, or a "one-handed" handshake as courteous but a "two-handed" handshake as overbearing. A mediator, then, must be attentive to such norms so as not to exacerbate tensions: where a mediator asks a party not to interrupt by placing her hand on a party's arm to suggest restraint, the mediator may have done something highly offensive; in working with an orthodox Muslim or Jew in a mediation session, a female mediator who holds out her hand for a farewell handshake may cause discomfort and embarrassment. Some of these cultural norms and practices a mediator can study and learn—and must do so; for others, one learns in the context, seeking guidance from the parties themselves as to how to proceed comfortably and respectfully.

A significant part of a mediator's job is to be a communicator and translator. When considering diversity dynamics, this means performing those tasks to build a bridge among cultures. Of course, as a mediator, one has her own culture, affiliations and traditions; they constitute the lens through which she sees the world and shapes the way in which she conducts the mediation. The mediator must persistently try to appreciate how her vision might be tinted by particular shades of culture and customs so that she can position herself to appreciate and understand the world as the disputants experience it. This is a lofty goal that is stated at a very high level of generality. But the mediator can take some concrete steps to advance it. What are they?

Mediator Chants for Constructive Interventions: 4 B's

The expert's advice to the recreational runner who is preparing to run her first marathon is that she should develop a thought, phrase, or chant—a mantra—that she can call upon in specific parts of the race to motivate and energize her performance. "I didn't train in order to quit" might be a phrase one runner chants when she feels like dropping out before reaching the finish; if she develops a chant for each mile, she might be heard repeating, "Mile 22, I am through with you."

A mediator needs a comparable set of phrases to remind us of the challenges that human diversity presents to conducting a constructive conversation. Here are four:

Be Aware

A mediator must study and understand her own cultural norms so as not to be a prisoner of them. Does she think that the person who speaks quickly and presents information in a readily organized manner is smarter than the person who speaks softly and meanders in her presentation?

Going further, is the mediator aware of how she, and others, might stereotype disputing participants, and the impact that one's implicit biases might have on the mediation dynamics?

Stereotypes are exaggerated and oversimplified generalizations about a group. When one envisions a "New Yorker" or a "German banker" or "a female lawyer," one could quickly develop negative *and* positive characteristics for particular members of these categories. The New Yorker, for example, is "smart and sophisticated but rude and impatient." The danger of stereotyping is that a person takes some (or all) of those characteristics and attributes those to the individual New Yorker who is participating in the mediation. When the New Yorker displays impatience, the mediator (or other parties) may think that is "just his being a New Yorker" rather than consider the possibility that he is not normally impatient but that he is today because he is worried about not being with his child who is seriously ill.

Implicit biases can undermine a mediator's neutrality. If the mediator is told that she will be mediating a case involving "gifted students" at the high school, then she might tend to begin her treatment of them in a way that assumes positive characteristics; conversely, if the mediator is told that she will be meeting with "the troublemakers," both she, and they, may think less positively about their own capacities and possibilities. A mediator, with reasonable effort, can target how a party's implicit biases are affecting the negotiating process and she can take steps to address those dynamics using standard BADGER tools. But it is much more difficult to appreciate how one's own behavior in these matters impact the discussion. The adage about "self-fulfilling prophecies" is accurate; they can make a negative or positive difference to the mediation, so a mediator's continuing challenge is to "be aware of" the prophecies she brings to the conversation.

Be Careful

A mediator must learn about the special needs of potential parties. Someone with learning disabilities may concentrate better in a room that is simple and plain with no distractions; someone who is visually impaired may need to have any documents ahead of time; someone with a stress-related disorder may need a time-out room.

Miscommunication is all too prevalent in every dispute. But where there are differences due to diversity, miscommunication and misunderstanding become even more likely.

When the mediator communicates, is her language riddled with culturally-based colloquial expressions that make it difficult to understand by persons outside that language group? Presume the mediation parties are two businesspersons, one of whom is a native English speaker and the other whose first language is Vietnamese, and that the mediator is a native English speaker who is conducting the mediation conference in English. The mediator, in a caucus with the businessperson whose first language is not English, wants to engage in some reality-testing by exploring whether the proposal that party is about to make might unnecessarily create settlement barriers, and she asks: "Do you think *going there might blow up in your face?*" That informal expression might be incomprehensible to a non-native English language speaker.

Does the mediator appreciate the fact that certain gestures have very different meanings in different cultures: does a "thumbs up" gesture mean "all is good" or could it mean an obscenity?

Where diversity of gender, race or ethnicity is a distinctive feature of the dispute, will having a co-mediation team that reflects a comparable diversity strengthen party trust and confidence in the process?

A mediator must be careful that her language and vocabulary is both respectful and comprehensible and she must pay attention to the meeting atmosphere she creates so that people feel safe, respected, and included.

Be Respectful

The values of people matter deeply to them. They must be acknowledged and worked with.

People go to different countries and cultures for recreation; they bring foreign artifacts home and appreciate them as art. They celebrate differences. A mediator should look to build on this natural appreciation.

And while we tend to emphasize that differences create conflicts, it is important to remember that sometimes differences in attitudes and beliefs towards a matter are the basis for making an agreement possible. A performing artist may be less comfortable taking financial risks than is a concert promoter. That difference in risk-taking may form the basis for the performer accepting a lower, but guaranteed, performance fee in exchange for the promoter retaining a larger percentage of revenue from ticket sales.

Build Trust

Building trust does not happen quickly or in a leap. It is built incrementally—and usually in small steps. Difference and diversity can generate distrust; people sometimes fear what they don't understand. It is crucial that the mediator be thoughtful about building trust. She must show people that she cares by listening thoughtfully and being interested in each party's culture. She must be reliable in performing terms of any commitments she makes, from sending promised documents to handling meeting arrangements. By modeling reliability, a mediator is in position to encourage others to be reliable themselves.

The Model Standards of Conduct for Mediators (Appendix) state that "cultural understandings" are a part of mediator competence. According to the International Mediation Institute in The Hague, such understanding includes: being able to appreciate similarities and differences between cultures; recognizing one's own cultural influences; and being able to understand the cultural perspective of mediation participants and optimize communication among them. At one level, of course, it is the height of human folly to believe that one can gain complete understanding of people with whom one interacts; human beings are simply too complex for that to happen. But at another level—a crucial one—that observation about how difficult it is does not serve as an acceptable excuse for a mediator not to do the hard work of trying to understand and interact effectively with persons of different backgrounds and cultures. A mediator has a professional responsibility to make her best effort to pay attention to, and learn about, how particular differences impact human interaction in a conflict setting.

13

Practical Challenges and Ethical Dilemmas

All true polishing is done by friction.

Mary Parker Follett

A mediator acts deliberately, not haphazardly. While BADGER provides a framework and guidelines for shaping mediator conduct, it is not an answer book.

Practice challenges and ethical dilemmas inevitably arise. Novel questions call for thoughtful responses. A mediator confronts many of these challenges on the firing line; she has very little time for contemplation—and she has only one chance to respond successfully. The stakes are high. That is what makes mediating so rewarding and its study so important.

This chapter presents 20 such challenges and dilemmas in a question-and-answer format. Where appropriate, an example illustrates the rationale for a particular answer.

1. Can mediation begin only after the negotiating parties have tried and failed to resolve their dispute?

Of course not. Mediation is a process for managing change. Disputants can anticipate conflict. Using a mediator earlier, rather than later, can reduce strife, minimize problems, lower disputing costs, and establish a framework for dealing constructively with issues that arise.

> *Example.* Federal budget cuts resulted in a 25% reduction of a state government's social service budget. With a smaller budget, the state

had to decide which programs for the elderly, homeless, disabled, and indigent populations it wanted to support and which to discontinue.

Initially, the state reduced the budgets for all affected programs by 25%. Such an across-the-board cut had a greater impact on small programs than on large ones. Some larger agencies could maintain programs by reallocating fixed overhead costs to other program budgets or by minimizing services; other agencies, however, were effectively incapacitated. Social service priorities were being determined, then, not by human needs but by organizational structure. Officials wanted to have the budget allocations follow the planning process, rather than *vice versa*.

With the governor's support, the commissioners of the 18 affected state agencies, representatives for the 168 town and local governments, and spokespersons for the more than 800 nonprofit service providers throughout the state brought in a mediator to help them negotiate the issues of which social services should be preserved, what their relative priority should be, and how much money they should receive. The mediator helped each team prepare for and conduct the negotiating sessions. Four months later, all parties signed an agreement.

We get the impression that we should use a mediator only after parties have failed to resolve their dispute by themselves and only when the costs of their not settling it are dramatic. There are certainly good reasons for using a mediator at that stage, but there is no compelling argument against using one at an earlier time.

2. Should a mediator agree to serve if the parties have unequal bargaining power?

It depends. This is a dangerously misleading question, and the mediator's response must be carefully crafted.

The concept of bargaining power is vague. Even if one can catalog various sources of power—wealth, guns, numbers of people, popularity, information, principles, natural resources, being in the majority group, subscribing to a certain religious faith, being articulate and persuasive, or an absence of competitors—no one can explicitly identify which source is most useful or how much of a particular source one must have in order to reach some threshold level for "having power." It is even more treacherous, then, to assess whether the parties' bargaining power is *equal* or *unequal*, for doing so assumes such things can be measured in a unitary calculus that tells us who has more.

Intuitively, however, we know that some people have more influence than others. Favorite punching bag examples are big business gouging hapless workers, professors intimidating students, and worldly husbands imposing lopsided divorce settlements on helpless wives. These stereotypes do hint at real-world problems that arise from unequal distribution of resources.

The mediator knows that every bargaining situation involves persons with different bargaining power. Before COMMITting oneself to serve as a mediator, a person must ask herself: Is the difference in bargaining power—economic, legal, experiential, political, or otherwise—so great that the more powerful party can simply dictate the outcome? If the answer is "yes," then she should not serve. Enshrining unilateral decision making in the legitimacy of collaborative problem solving is a sham that no mediator should endorse.

This answer is good in theory, but it is difficult in practice to spot a situation involving such extreme power imbalance. Frequently, relative power shifts from issue to issue and at different points in time. One party has more power when dealing with financial issues; another seems to have an upper hand when concerns about relational issues are raised. Or, in a multi-session mediation, one party arrives seemingly depressed and dispirited—ready to "cave in"; the other seems energetic and powerful. On another day, or after a break, this disparity disappears. How should a mediator proceed?

She must explore with the parties what has happened PRIOR-TO her entry. She must determine the parties' wishes with respect to proceeding. If all the parties believe that mediated discussions represent their best option for advancing their interests, then doubts about apparent disparities in bargaining power should be resolved in favor of respecting the parties' wishes to proceed.

> *Example.* In the case described above, numerous observers commented that the representatives of the nonprofit agencies were less capable as compared to the state's negotiators. These critics felt that the nonprofits had no leverage and were at the mercy of their counterparts in acquiring necessary information. They insisted that mediation be stopped. But the parties wanted to proceed. Accordingly, the mediator went forward, and the final agreement, endorsed by all participants, dramatically changed decision-making about social services delivery throughout the state.

Power disparities that make mediated discussions inappropriate are obvious and blatant. A battered spouse should not engage in mediated discussions with the perpetrator without independent representation or other protections in place; a single, impoverished migrant worker who works a twelve-hour day and lives in squalid employee housing quarters will not secure his interests through mediated negotiations with his menacing foreman. The mediator knows that mediation is a process for fostering independent decision-making. In a situation in which one party lacks the capacity to act independently (for fear of physical retaliation, inebriation, or minimal verbal or analytical skills), then the mediator should prevent the process from going forward.

Sometimes these disparities do not appear until the parties are engaged in the discussions. What should the mediator do then? The answer is straightforward: stop participating, but exit without a public denunciation. The mediator discharges the scapegoat task by informing the parties that in light of the way the discussions have progressed, she no longer believes she is able to serve them effectively—and she ends the mediation.

3. Is the mediator responsible for the quality of the parties' agreement?

No. But that response must not be misunderstood.

The agreement—and its quality—are a product of party deliberation and choice. The mediator must conduct the process to insure that the parties have examined a variety of perspectives, consulted relevant principles and norms, and worked to make their agreement as doable and durable as possible. The mediator does not, however, dictate party outcomes nor veto party preferences for failing to meet the mediator's evaluation of a desirable resolution.

When a mediator COMMITs to serve, she is dedicating herself to lead a process in which party self-determination and participatory decision-making resolve matters in dispute. If the individual mediator, or program designer contemplating the use of mediation, has any doubts about the desirability of resolving a controversy through mediated discussions, then she should resolve that question before, not after, agreeing to serve. For instance, suppose an individual employee wants to resolve an employment discrimination claim against a powerful employer through mediated discussions rather than by initiating a lawsuit. Should an individual agree to serve as a mediator? The mediator has every right to determine whether her own commitment to eradicating discriminatory treatment is consistent with encouraging the private settlement of such individual charges. She must take into account the possibility that the employee might agree to settlement terms less favorable than those that might be obtained by prevailing in a lawsuit; she must evaluate the benefits of the parties having prompt access to a dispute resolution process against the costs of possibly losing a valuable precedent in court. But once she decides to serve as mediator, the primary goal is to assist the parties reach a settlement on terms they find acceptable. Only if parties propose terms that are illegal or at odds with fundamental values that supported the mediator's original commitment to serve should the mediator let her own preferences become decisive and bring the discussion to a close.

Where parties decide, given their priorities, that particular terms are acceptable, the mediator should question those terms only to insure that they promote or secure the parties' interests. That a party might have gained more in a lawsuit or that the course of action differs from prevailing customs or the mediator's belief-system is irrelevant. Similarly, if the parties determine that they would rather have no agreement at all than adopt any of the settlement terms they have considered, that is fine. The mediator's job, without apology, is to deploy every element of BADGER to enhance informed decision making, spark creativity, and increase the likelihood of the parties developing an acceptable settlement.

It is important to appreciate the difference between a mediator who does not participate in mediated discussions because she concludes that the difference in bargaining power among the parties is so skewed that one party is unable to participate competently in making joint decisions from the situation in which the mediator tries to stop the mediated discussions because the parties are about to accept settlement terms that the mediator personally disapproves of or believes fall short of meeting such laudable goals as efficiency, wisdom, or maximizing the general well-being of others. The former is appropriate; the latter oversteps the mediator's role.

4. Can a mediator be neutral?

Yes. The mediator must have no preference that particular negotiating issues be resolved one way rather than another. Consider the following range of negotiating issues:

- A teachers' union and school district are deadlocked in their negotiations over whether the district can assign a teacher to more than two schools during the day, thereby necessitating multiple trips by the affected personnel.
- A parent and fifteen-year-old son disagree about what time the son must return home following the school dance.
- A social worker and youth counselor disagree over whether a child should be denied weekend visitation privileges with his family as a disciplinary measure for having refused to eat dinner at the institutional home.

It is certainly possible to find individuals capable of serving as mediators for these situations who have no preference that the matters be resolved in a particular way. That is sufficient to meet the standard of neutrality. The importance of remaining neutral cannot be overemphasized. If the mediator is not neutral, then one party will believe—correctly—that she is at an immediate disadvantage; the mediator and the other party are ganging up on her. That is not a formula for generating a successful resolution.

It is difficult to remain neutral. A mediator who sees an individual about to agree to terms that are less favorable than those possibly available in court is particularly prone to steering discussions in one party's favor. People have great difficulty in letting others decide for themselves how they want to live, but paternalistic attitudes are inconsistent with effectively conducting mediated discussions.

Mediators must be realistic about the extent of their neutrality. No thinking person can be neutral on every possible negotiating issue. People have definite convictions about educational programs, public safety policies, energy plans, abortion, affirmative action, and a host of other challenges that confront us in our personal and social environment. There is no reason to apologize for one's strong convictions; all one must acknowledge is that having such convictions disqualifies her from being a mediator in disputes involving those issues. Since no one is neutral about all possible negotiating issues or negotiating parties, no one can plausibly represent herself as being able to mediate all disputes.

> *Example.* A parent and a neighbor are disputing about the neighbor's conduct with the parent's child. The neighbor, who is in his early twenties, regularly offers drinks to the parent's teenage son, while the two hang out together. The parent is concerned about her son's drinking, which has resulted in his dropping out of school. The neighbor feels the parent is way too strict and uptight, which has caused (in his mind) the son's problem. The mediator herself has been through an addiction problem with a close family member and wants to "drill a set of brains" for the neighbor who is illegally offering alcohol to a minor. The mediator is not able to be neutral with respect to the issue of drinking; if that is the central issue in controversy, she should withdraw from continuing service.

Being perceived as neutral is as important as being neutral. For example, a professor who serves as a judge of a moot court competition in which a student from her school competes may be accused of favoring her student; the temptation to do so is understandable. The reverse is often true as well: a teacher, trying particularly hard not to be seen as playing favorites, may systematically ignore or undervalue her own student's interest. The lesson is simple: don't be a mediator in a situation in which one has a close personal or professional relationship with one of the parties.

Note that there is a close relationship between neutrality and impartiality. Impartiality often means freedom from favoritism, bias or prejudice. Impartiality requires a mediator to treat parties in an even-handed manner; for example, she must provide each party with an equally comfortable chair, sustain equal eye contact with them, provide all with an opportunity to speak, and meet with each party when conducting a caucus. This functional equality is, in many ways, easier to monitor than a mediator's duty to be neutral with respect to outcome.

5. Should a mediator be active or passive?

Neither. The question poses a false dichotomy. A mediator should do her job—BADGER the parties. Whether she does it loudly or quietly, is theatrical or understated, is a matter of individual style, not strategy. When people envision an active mediator, they think of someone who urges people to reconsider their perspectives and positions, prods people to move, and throws out ideas for settlement when the conversation is stuck. That is what mediators do. What varies from dispute to dispute are the specific strategies or the particular combination of techniques that the mediator adopts. How the mediator executes those aspects of her role is dictated not by whether she is active or passive but by the nature of the negotiating issues, the degree of rigidity in the parties' negotiating stance, and her own personal style.

6. Should a mediator identify "new" negotiating issues if the parties have not raised them themselves?

No, unless doing so is necessary to make certain that the parties can implement their agreement or to help parties pass successfully from the more fluid, formative stage of their negotiation process to its more tangible, substantive component.

A mediator must not hesitate to identify additional matters that, if not addressed and resolved, will jeopardize compliance with the agreement. If Smith agrees to pay Jones $350 for the repair of Jones' bicycle that Smith damaged, but no one says anything about when or how the payment will be made, the mediator must raise those issues. Otherwise, compliance is jeopardized.

If the mediator enters the discussions before the parties have developed an agenda of negotiating issues, she can suggest additional issues for the parties to address if doing so will stabilize their negotiating relationship or expand their negotiating flexibility.

Example. A group of Native Americans took physical possession of a private campsite that was contiguous to the Adirondack State Park in New York State. They demanded that the state grant the Native Americans clear legal title of the entire park; the state refused.

The parties existed in an uneasy alliance for months. State police officers had multiple surveillance points around the campsite; the occupants had 24-hour guards packing guns. Legal charges of all sorts were thrown at the land occupants, but no change resulted. Meanwhile, neighboring residents had to pass the campsite going to and from a popular lodge. One evening, a family left the lodge and drove past the campsite on their way to town. A shot was fired. The bullet traveled through the trunk of the car into the back seat and hit a ten-year-old girl, who survived but was completely paralyzed.

Fear mounted, rhetoric escalated, and demands for action increased. Rumors abounded; citizens reported that reliable sources said that a group of four hundred armed Native Americans from South Dakota had been seen passing through Chicago on their way to the campsite in New York; twelve hours elapsed before the sheer idiocy of that rumor was laid to rest. The citizens wanted the Native Americans to leave; the Native Americans wanted title to the land. County officials wanted to prosecute individuals for a variety of criminal offenses, and politicians were clamoring for action. At that juncture, mediators arrived.

After meeting and talking with the various stakeholders and gaining an understanding of their aspirations, the mediators proposed that the parties develop negotiating proposals regarding a rumor control mechanism. No one had previously identified this as an agenda item for negotiation. No one pretended that it would resolve the more substantive concerns, but everyone agreed that the urgency of the situation demanded a short-term, tangible, and effective device for minimizing miscalculations and stabilizing various relationships. A procedure was promptly negotiated. The successful resolution of rumor control mechanisms developed both momentum for and investment in further discussions.

7. What if parties, during the mediated discussions, act in uncooperative or disruptive ways—interrupting, calling each other names, or threatening one another?

A mediator must move quickly and decisively to insure such exchanges do not result in a downward destructive spiral, fully appreciative of the fact that such behavior is not unusual and comes naturally to parties locked in a conflict.

The basic principle guiding the mediator's response to such behavior is straightforward: mediation requires everyone to agree to the outcome. The use of abusive language is personally offensive and disrespectful; it generates a defensive response from those at whom it is directed, making accommodation much more difficult to achieve. Words like "slumlords," "pigs," and "welfare bums" inflame reactions rather than gain cooperation. Threats—particularly threats of violence—do the same thing.

If parties malign each other's character, the mediator raises communication as an issue and perhaps proposes that they address each other by name or title. If someone threatens violence, the mediator declares a caucus and meets first with that party; she forcefully tells the party that the threats must stop for mediated discussions to proceed. Threats to commit acts of violence undermine the integrity of any possible agreement and make it useless for people to continue talking.

A mediator must be patient, non-defensive, and willing to be the scapegoat of the parties' vehemence and tirades. But the types of conduct noted here do more than challenge the mediator's good will; they are direct attacks on the principles of treating one another with respect and dignity that shape collaborative resolution through discussion. The mediator, as the guardian of the process, must do that which enables meaningful conversation to proceed. If the parties cannot act within this basic structure, then the mediator must protect the integrity of the process by bringing the discussion to a halt.

8. What if parties ask the mediator for her assessment of whether a particular offer of settlement is fair or reasonable?

Don't give it. A party always tries to gain mediator support, wanting the mediator to agree that its proposal is fair or reasonable or that the party is acting "in good faith." The mediator must resist all such attempts. Consider the consequences.

If the mediator agrees that a party's offer is "reasonable" or "fair"—for instance, that the employer's offer to increase wages by an amount equal to the cost of living is "reasonable"—then any proposal that exceeds that figure will automatically be labeled "unreasonable." No longer is it simply the employer alone who believes that the union's proposal to increase wages by 6% is "unreasonable" when the cost of living has increased by less than 4%; now, the employer can gloat, even the "impartial, objective" mediator believes a 6% increase is "off the wall."

The mediator's response to such endorsement requests must be prompt and uniform. She must put the responsibility right back in the parties' laps. Her response would be: "It is not important whether I believe the proposal is reasonable. The question is whether it is an arrangement that the two of you endorse."

There may come a time, however, when the parties are completely frustrated and want the mediator's best judgment as to what the settlement terms should be.

9. Should a mediator ever make a formal "mediator's proposal" for settlement?

Yes, but only if she is asked to do so by all parties and only after she has exhausted every other means to find an accord.

A mediator's proposal is a formal recommendation of how unresolved issues should be settled. The goal of such a proposal is to recommend terms that the parties will accept. If the proposal is successful, parties adopt the recommendations as a package and a resolution is secured.

A mediator resists the request to make formal settlement proposals for very practical reasons. First, parties often ask for the mediator's assessment early in the discussions; to give it to them at that point short-circuits the negotiation process, undermines the principle that parties must take responsibility for resolving their disputes, and puts the mediator in the posture of making recommendations that are not grounded in an enriched understanding of the parties' interests and history. Second, advice is cheap. Helping people resolve their concerns requires effort. If the mediator's effort to help others resolve their dispute is to succeed, then she must become immersed in the dynamics of the dispute and engaged in the discussion and settlement-building process; offering solutions too quickly converts a mediator into a consultant. Finally, people tend to comply with settlement terms if they have played a meaningful role in developing them. Having to live according to terms that an outsider has proposed can be an irritating insult to a party's independence.

When the mediator makes the proposal, she is not stating what she personally believes is a "fair" or "reasonable" resolution of the particular matters. Rather, she takes what she has learned from the parties in their joint sessions and caucuses; considers their respective needs, interests, and constraints; and proposes specific settlement terms that she believes the parties will accept. The mediator does not try to act as a judge by determining the rights and duties of the parties, nor does she try to split everything in half. Instead, the mediator tries to shape a future relationship that is workable and responsive to their most important interests and concerns.

Once the mediator makes a proposal, she may not be viewed as neutral by the parties and her usefulness will be severely restricted, if not eliminated. If the parties accept the proposal, fine; if they alter only limited aspects of it, the mediator can help them do so. But if the parties do not adopt her major recommendations or a substantial number of them, then they probably will not trust her subsequent efforts to help them reach an agreement, for they will justifiably believe her to be an advocate for her own proposals rather than a neutral. The party who feels disfavored by the proposal may storm out. Given that reality, a mediator makes a formal settlement proposal only after: she has BADGERed the parties to explore all other avenues for settlement; all the parties request it; she explains the goal of her proposal is acceptability; and she warns the parties that she may not be useful to them as a mediator after making her recommendation.

The one context in which the mediator's formal proposal is very useful and certain to be adopted is when the proposal simply recommends settlement terms that the parties have privately indicated they will accept. Sometimes the parties need a scapegoat or punching bag in order to settle; they need to advise their constituents that they agreed to proposals advanced by a neutral party but did not cave in to their counterpart's proposal. The mediator's formal proposal satisfies that need perfectly.

10. What does a mediator do if the parties have reached impasse?

She has them examine the costs of not settling. If alternatives to negotiable options appear more attractive to one or more parties, there will be no settlement and the discussions will terminate. That may seem too easy a response to such an important challenge. But the response is correct; it is the challenge that has been miscast. The crucial assessment that the mediator must make is not what strategy the mediator should employ if the parties reach impasse but rather, are the parties really at an impasse?

Our conventional image of people at an impasse is that they are deadlocked on some matters. They have exchanged proposals and ideas, perhaps even made some compromises, but now they refuse to budge from their announced positions. They may play brinksmanship with each other or break off discussions and pursue independent courses of action to protect their interests. This conventional image of impasse is misleading. Instead, the mediator must view the concept of impasse as a continuum. An impasse does not exist simply because people have proposed incompatible solutions to various negotiating issues. Otherwise, parties would reach impasse the moment they offered different solutions to the various issues in dispute. The key criterion for determining whether impasse exists is the degree to which a party is committed to pursuing non-negotiated solutions if its preferred solution is not adopted.

Looking at the concept of impasse from this perspective generates two conclusions: first, in some contexts, parties can reach impasse very rapidly; second, the greater one party's need to secure the other's cooperation in order to achieve its own goals—the more they are "married" to one another—the less likely it is that they will ever really reach an impasse (even if they claim to be at that point).

Consider the following examples.

> *Example 1.* Anna Montalvo, a recent recipient of an MBA degree, wants to pursue a career in human resource management. She interviews with Elena Durham for an entry-level personnel position in a large, well-known department store. Two weeks later, Durham telephones Montalvo and offers her a position; the annual salary is $45,000, and the position requires that she work every weekend. Montalvo decides to negotiate. She indicates to Durham that she can accept the position only if the beginning salary is $50,000 and she does not have to work on weekends. Durham counters by stating that her bottom line is a starting salary of $46,500 and a promise to consider changing Montalvo's schedule after 6 months of employment. Montalvo responds that she cannot take the job for a salary less than $47,500. Durham reacts by withdrawing the job offer and hanging up.

> *Example 2.* A school board engages in negotiations with the teachers' union; there are 700 teachers in the public school system, which serves 10,000 students. The school board proposes a salary increase of 3.5% for each year of a 2-year contract and demands that the individual teacher pay the entire amount of any future premium increases in the health insurance plan; the union counters by proposing a 6% salary increase for each year of a 2-year contract, an expansion of employer-paid health insurance benefits to include dental coverage, and an increase in the number of teachers who can take sabbatical leave from the current level of 3 teachers per year to a new maximum of 7 teachers per year. Six months later, neither party has modified any of its proposals; their present contract is about to expire. Both parties declare that they have reached an impasse.

In *Example 1*, the employer and the job candidate quickly reached an impasse. Montalvo apparently decided that the employer's last offer was not sufficiently attractive and chose to make a counterproposal that Durham quickly rejected. Had a mediator been present, she might have caucused with Montalvo to insure that she considered the consequences of not reducing her salary demands: the time she would spend looking elsewhere for employment; the lost opportunity to acquire competent training and pursue a well-defined career track in an established, reputable company; and the like. If Montalvo believed she could do better elsewhere, she would take the risk and proceed, as she did, to make a counterproposal.

This type of transaction is a typical event in our daily lives. We often reach impasse over some issue—often money—and quickly move on. We don't pursue the discussion because we believe we can get what we want elsewhere. But if what we are seeking is scarce and only our negotiating counterpart can provide it to us, then our mobility is restricted. We must find a way to gain a settlement.

That is the dynamic operating in the second example. The parties claim they are at impasse, but they really are not. They may be stuck; they may break off discussions for a while. But what are their options to reaching settlement? The board cannot close down the school system, as a private employer might close down her business. And unlike an individual conducting a job search, the teachers cannot leave *en masse* to work for another employer. In a very practical sense, the parties must reach an agreement. That does not mean, of course, that the process of doing so may not be strewn with grief, anger, harsh words, work stoppages, and the like. Ultimately, however, the parties must continue to live with one another—ideally they will strike a deal.

A mediator analyzes two elements when assessing whether the parties have reached impasse. First, she examines whether the parties have a relationship such that nonnegotiated solutions are a practical alternative. Second, she examines the parties' stated and unstated positions to see whether she can detect any flexibility in them.

The mediator wants to analyze the parties' relationship to determine their relative degree of interdependence; the higher it is, the less likely that they will reach impasse. Parties do not need to be "married" to each other in order for their relationship at a particular time to be such that they have no practical alternative to working out an acceptable solution. Two co-workers may detest each other; each might be looking elsewhere for employment. But if neither can afford to be unemployed and each wants to continue to receive favorable performance reviews, then their supervisor should be able to BADGER them into finding a way to overcome their "incompatible work styles" and complete the assignment that requires their working together.

The stronger the interdependence among the parties, the more susceptible they are to being persuaded to find an acceptable resolution. That should prod the mediator to redouble her efforts to generate movement from the parties. She has an arsenal of persuasive techniques at her disposal, and she must try them repeatedly. She must probe for the slightest hint of flexibility by re-examining the parties' stated and unstated priorities, reviewing the facts and their ambiguities, studying the language in which proposed settlement terms are couched, and monitoring the rate and extent of concessions and counter offers that the parties have made. Before appealing to the costs of not settling, the mediator must be certain she has accurately read each party's movements and appreciates its constraints. She must not hesitate to acknowledge an impasse if it arises, but, more than anyone else, she must not do so precipitously. The parties and observers quickly become discouraged by apparently clashing, immobilized public positions; the mediator must be more subtle and persistent.

Whatever the parties say about their fixed positions, "impasse" is only reached when everyone walks away.

> *Example 3.* A mediation concerning the break-up of a business partnership began in the afternoon and proceeded to nearly midnight. There were many issues to address: division of property, allocation of expected revenues, use of customer lists, future competition, use of business name, and potential liability for past acts. At 11:50 p.m., with no movement on any issue, the mediator called for a close to the session, stating that she was sorry she was unable to assist the parties resolve their concerns but the building was going to close in ten minutes. Before midnight, every issue had been resolved. The parties had moved internally but had not been ready to show their flexibility until the deadline was announced.

11. What should the mediator do if she learns, as a result of caucusing with the parties, that there is overlap in what the parties are willing to settle on?

Use that knowledge to get a settlement. The ethical dilemma is more apparent than real.

This challenge arises only because the mediator chose to caucus. Suppose a landlord tells the mediator in caucus that she would accept $1,000 for settlement of the rent arrears rather than the $3,000 she has been demanding; then, when the mediator caucuses with the tenant, the tenant volunteers to pay $1,500 in order to settle the matter. Only the mediator knows about this $500 overlap. What should she do?

She must immediately realize that she has been given leverage for gaining settlement on any outstanding unresolved issues. For instance, if the landlord refuses to fix the tenant's stove until she receives payment for the rent due, the mediator might persuade her to fix the appliance immediately in return for getting more than $1,000 from the tenant. The mediator can pursue that line of inquiry because of additional resources with which she has to work.

When the only unresolved issue is payment of rent arrears, the mediator faces a dilemma: she will determine who gets the $500 windfall by deciding which party speaks first when they reconvene. Whichever party she asks to speak first will forfeit $500. The easiest way to avoid the dilemma is for the mediator to bring the parties together and indicate that there is an agreement in principle on how to solve the one remaining item; then, assuming she has obtained the parties' permission to do so, the mediator can tell them what each is willing to do about the rent arrears and then let the parties resolve the difference themselves. Alternatively, though less supportive of party autonomy, the mediator could bring the parties together, mention that in private discussions each had indicated a willingness to settle at figures that were mutually acceptable, and then, presuming party permission to use the information she gained in caucus, suggest that they settle on the sum of $1,250 to resolve the issue of rent arrears. Some persons view this latter approach as manipulative, but sometimes it is appropriate in order to secure commitments.

12. How firm and detailed must mediated agreements be?

The need for precision varies with the situation. Clarity is important, but the mediator must not paralyze the parties from acting by insisting on a phantom certainty.

Most people think that when parties agree on certain matters, everyone knows what has been "offered" and "accepted." A negotiated agreement, however, is more fluid than that image suggests. Some terms of agreement are constitutionally vague: neighbors agree not to "bother" each other; parents agree to "respect" their teenager's privacy; teachers agree to develop a make-up exam that will "fairly" test a student's knowledge of the subject matter and will be "no more difficult" than the exam originally given; employers agree to terminate employees only if there is "just cause." What have these people actually agreed to do? These terms and concepts are not meaningless, but they are subject to varying, and conflicting, interpretations. A mediator must not block such terms of agreement simply because they are vague; they may be as precise as the subject matter allows, or their use may reflect a deliberate decision by the parties to postpone their attempts to agree on a more precise meaning.

Some oral commitments consist of a simple assertion: "Don't worry—I'll take care of that in my own way." Any party who accepts such a representation is trusting the speaker to respond to the situation without knowing exactly what the speaker will do. Unless the mediator believes such uncertainty jeopardizes compliance with the agreement, she should not be disturbed by the fact that there is not one explicit solution corresponding to each formulated issue; the absence of logical symmetry need not diminish the integrity of the agreement.

Some persons insist on certain terms of agreement as a face-saving measure, knowing even when they make the demand that subsequent events will render compliance with such terms infeasible. Divorcing spouses might insist on a provision that guarantees their infant children the right to choose their custodial parent upon reaching the age of fifteen. But if the children's schooling, friends, and related activities for ten years will center around the environment of one custodial parent, then the likelihood that the children will "really" make such a choice is minimal; the noncustodial parent realizes this, will not contest it when it occurs, but insists on including such a provision so that he or she can assure the children that neither parent ever abandoned them.

A mediator cannot fall into the trap of believing—and then insisting—that a mediated agreement must embody a detailed plan of action that anticipates and makes provision for resolving all future contingencies. To assess an agreement against such a standard is to grasp for certainty in an uncertain world. A mediated agreement must be developed with an appreciation for the diversity and unpredictability of life's experiences; that means some aspects of it will simply be a road map for future action, rather than a finely detailed prescription.

Acknowledging the role and value of ambiguities and uncertainties is not to excuse sloppiness when precision is possible. It does, however, prevent us from being lulled into the false belief that reaching an agreement automatically entails a problem-free future.

13. Should a mediator agree to assume a formal role in the implementation of the agreement if the parties so request?

Where possible, no. A mediator must be a catalyst in spurring parties to reach agreement; she must not be an ever-present crutch for them.

At least four problems arise when a mediator assumes an integral role in the implementation of the settlement. First, the neutrality expected of a mediator can be incompatible with the role of a compliance officer. Making the transition from a facilitating posture to a monitoring role is particularly difficult where parties appropriately do not view the mediator as the authoritative figure that the role of compliance officer requires.

Second, if the people responsible for implementing the agreement are the same as those who developed it, they may tend unproductively to revisit with the mediator what happened in the mediation. Focusing on the past rather than the future can impede the effective implementation of the agreement.

Third, if the people implementing the agreement were not participants in the mediation, they may understandably want the mediator to "clarify" the various terms to which the bargaining parties agreed. Often, for example, representatives of an employer and a union negotiate an agreement that personnel at the building or local level are responsible for implementing, or leaders of a community organization negotiate with officials of a private corporation to establish a summer employment program for local youths and lower-echelon personnel from both organizations are charged with implementing the program. In such situations, the new players need to develop their own dynamics of interaction. They need to take charge of the terms of agreement and create a shared understanding of their meaning. If the mediator is viewed by these participants as the expert who can clarify the original intent of a particular term or clause, that developing synergy among the parties is disrupted and the mediator is converted into an umpire.

Finally, if the mediator anticipates having the role of compliance officer, she may be unproductively cautious in doing her job. A mediator takes risks when prodding parties to consider their interests and reconsider their positions. She cannot constrain her efforts for fear that she will undermine her effectiveness during the implementation phase. A mediator is not irreplaceable; others can monitor the agreement.

There is, of course, another way in which the mediator might be asked to participate in implementing the agreement: the parties might ask the mediator to participate because she has the requisite expertise that the parties have agreed to obtain as part of their agreement. Suppose the parties to the mediated discussion agree to hire an investment counselor to help them analyze their portfolio; presume also that the person serving as the mediator is a professional investment counselor. The parties trust her and ask her to be the investment counselor that they are committed to obtaining. Should she agree to serve? Absolutely not. No one is indispensable. The mediator may be the acknowledged expert in a particular professional field. If she chooses to serve as a mediator, however, she must not use that role as a conduit for obtaining other business. Otherwise, no party could ever be certain that a mediator was prodding them toward settlement terms that matched their priorities rather than the mediator's business needs.

14. Must all mediated discussions take place in private?

No. Private discussions (often coupled with confidentiality) usually encourage freer communication among parties and promote settlement-building. Inhibitions generated by a curious crowd or concerns about public reactions are minimized if discussions are private. Reasons often cited for privacy include:

- There may be competitive or confidential information that cannot be discussed publicly but must be shared in order for parties to appreciate the constraints under which everyone is operating.
- If an agreement requires approval by a negotiator's constituency, then the negotiator wants to present the tentative agreement to her membership in the manner most conducive to reasoned debate and careful deliberation. But if various aspects of the agreement are reported publicly before such a presentation is made, the chance to set the context for the ensuing debate is lost.
- If aspects of the agreement are publicly reported as being settled, and a party's constituency is upset by those terms, it may force its negotiating team to adopt a more rigid posture on the remaining items as a way of retaliating for the earlier concessions.
- Discussions, by their very nature, must be fluid, with some items being resolved only tentatively until others are definitively settled; public reporting of "agreements" often neglects that distinction and forces the negotiators to explain why certain "agreements" no longer exist.
- Conducting mediated discussions in public encourages nonproductive histrionics and speech making by the parties, reduces all discussions in public to a "report" of each party's present position, and removes the "real mediating and negotiating" to the back rooms and telephones.

These are important insights. They are not, however, always applicable or accurate. Mediation is used in a variety of contexts. For mediated discussions involving such public issues as budget allocations, industrial development as it impacts public park lands, or siting toxic waste disposal plants, compelling reasons support a presumption in favor of conducting them in public. Having the discussions open to public observation can provide an incentive for parties to prepare thoroughly and conduct themselves in an exemplary fashion; contrary to the expressed concern that negotiators will grandstand for their constituencies, parties do not want to embarrass themselves by appearing poorly prepared, uninformed, obstinate, or unreasonable. The public nature of the proceeding forces parties to depersonalize their comments, more so than in private exchanges; this in itself contributes to the settlement-building process. If members of a negotiating team need time to talk among themselves, they can always use private caucuses; but citizens should witness how the results of those deliberations are incorporated into the ensuing discussions so that they are confident that caucuses do not become merely an avenue for parties to avoid public accountability.

Conducting mediated discussions in a public forum is comparable to conducting courtroom trials in open session. In certain cases, the public should have the right to observe what transpires in mediated discussions and to evaluate the issues in dispute, the quality of their resolution, and the manner in which all participants—parties and mediator alike—operate. Mediation must not be shrouded in mystery. If the public does not understand why the participants in mediated discussions do the things they do, that only underscores the need for more public education about the dynamics of those processes and more public access to them. There are compelling arguments for restricting some sessions, or some types of mediated discussions, from public view. In a democratic society, other situations favor an open forum.

15. Should mediators be licensed?

No, at least not at present. All of us act as mediators in our roles as parent, friend, supervisor, co-worker, teacher, neighbor, and citizen. Requiring everyone to have a license to do so is as silly as requiring a license to cook or spell.

Licensing procedures not only restrict entry into a particular service, but are often tied to requiring the candidate to be trained in a certain way—for example, by obtaining a degree in an accredited college or graduate program or to have served a minimum number of years in a related profession. Mediation is far too diverse, fertile and new a field—drawing from many different disciplines—to benefit from such restrictions, at least at present. Unanswered questions remain. Should law or psychology or other disciplines dominate the curriculum? How can performance-based criteria be developed and administered without being cost-prohibitive?

Despite the challenges of licensing, those mediating as a profession or in public programs must have adequate training. Many institutions, including community centers and court panels, require that mediators have a certain number of hours of training (ranging from 25 to 40 hours), experience mediating and co-mediating cases with a mentor giving guidance, participate in continuing education, and undergo performace review through participant evaluation feedback or program personnel assessment. Such requirements qualify the mediator to be certified to serve on the center or court panel.

A related question is whether a mediator needs process or substantive expertise. Can a person who capably mediates collective bargaining agreements transfer her process skills so as to mediate divorce cases? Being a process expert is not always a sufficient condition for being an effective mediator.

The question then arises: What subject matters must a mediator be knowledgeable about? To understand and execute the basic elements of BADGER requires an analytical understanding of such concepts as conflict, power, trust, representation, approaches to bargaining, as well as an appreciation of motivation, psychological barriers to settlement and communication theory. To that she must add an understanding of the various dimensions of the subject matter in dispute. But it is not reasonable to expect one individual to be conversant in all matters that bear upon the subject matter in dispute; one dispute—for instance, between tobacco industry representatives and government health officials—might require expertise in such diverse areas as political theory and operations, law, economics, psychology, accounting, advertising, chemistry, biology, computer science, and history. No one can be an expert in all these matters, nor is such expertise necessary in order to mediate effectively. Being knowledgeable in some of these areas, however, is essential for being an effective mediator; the areas of expertise that are most useful should be left to the parties to decide when they select their mediator. This leads to the next question.

16. When should co-mediation be considered?

Whenever resources allow. Having a team comprised of two or more mediators can serve many purposes. In a divorce mediation, for example, having female and male mediators who respectively have law and mental health backgrounds can be helpful—both for gender balance and for bringing in relevant knowledge from two professional fields. Sometimes, one proposed mediator has process expertise but lacks substantive expertise and can constructively partner with someone who has relevant knowledge in the subject matter of the dispute—intellectual property, securities, or international trade. An apprentice mediator can productively partner with a seasoned mediator for training purposes. Often, ethnic or religious diversity is helpful on a mediation team.

The synergy of two mediators offers a variety of advantages. Compared to a solo mediator, two mediators can offer twice the listening capacity; the insights and expertise; the opportunity for parties to make meaningful connections; the patience and stamina; and the creative potential. Two mediators can model constructive modes of communication and decision-making. Two mediators can make the mediation more efficient by dividing up tasks—one mediator can work on the agreement, for example, while the other continues to wrap up a final issue. A team can also learn from one another.

On the other hand, co-mediation can be fraught with tensions and difficulties. If the two mediators are not "in synch," there is the possibility for unproductive competition, for a less dominant mediator to feel "side-lined," for the mediation to take longer due to difficulty in making decisions, and for efforts to be made that pull the mediation in different directions. Two heads can be worse than one.

To be effective in serving the parties, a co-mediation team must share the same philosophy and approach. Do both believe, for example, that parties should participate if possible? That a caucus should be used only if necessary? That mediators should not give evaluations or make proposals? If co-mediators share similar perspectives on these matters, they can render significant, efficient service to the parties; if they disagree, they generate process inefficiencies and, quite possibly, significant party frustration.

17. If one or more participants do not speak the language in which the mediation is being conducted, should an interpreter be used?

Yes. Mediation is a process to enhance communication and understanding. It is critical that everyone understand what is being said. A professional interpreter means that the interpreter—like the mediator—will be neutral and will not selectively translate what has been said or re-frame and re-interpret parties' remarks.

A skilled interpreter can provide simultaneous translation so that she translates as a party speaks, just a beat behind. This allows for conversations to proceed in a natural manner. Where accuracy is critical, the interpreter might use consecutive translation, allowing a speaker to complete a sentence or a thought before interpreting.

The interpreter is there for all participants to fully understand the proceedings—for the person who does not speak the language that the mediation is being conducted in, but, equally important, for others to understand that person too. The parties should be encouraged not to speak to the interpreter, but rather to speak to one another with the interpreter enabling comprehension of what is said by all to all.

A practical danger in many mediation settings is that a party's "best friend" is the only "language interpreter" available. In such instances, a mediator proceeds cautiously, gently prodding the "advocate's interpreter" to provide as objective a translation as is possible while acknowledging the difficulty for that person to distance herself intellectually and emotionally from the substantive controversy.

18. Does a mediator have a duty to make certain that a party makes a decision based on complete information?

No. It is easy to envision situations in which this response places a mediator in an uncomfortable bind. What if the mediator learns that the statute of limitations has run on a plaintiff's claim, thereby preventing the plaintiff from obtaining any recovery in a lawsuit, and the plaintiff just turned down a $30,000 offer from the defendant? Should the mediator advise the plaintiff that she is lucky to have that offer—she'd best take it? Should the mediator warn the defendant?

On the one hand, the mediator would prefer parties to be as informed as possible about relevant aspects of their dispute. Here, the statute of limitations is a critical piece of information. On the other hand, the mediator should not be providing legal advice—whether or not the mediator is a lawyer, she is not acting in that capacity when she mediates. Additionally, where the "advice" favors one party over another, it impacts neutrality.

Certainly, a mediator could counsel parties in this situation to get legal— or other professional—advice as they consider offers (if they haven't done that already). The mediator can explore issues and concerns that have been raised about various matters in dispute. However, the mediator should not give affirmative advice about the law's impact on the dispute. Whether or not a statute of limitations has expired appears to be a simple question. In application, it can be devilishly tricky, and is a matter that is regularly litigated. The mediator should not give an opinion.

19. Should the mediator give legal (or other professional) advice she is qualified to give when the parties request that service?

This question requires an importantly nuanced response. A mediator is sometimes asked for her legal—or therapeutic—opinion on a particular matter. When that happens, a mediator should remind the parties about her role as a neutral facilitator. The job of a neutral expert, arbiter, lawyer or counselor is strikingly different from that of a mediator, and many reasons argue for not mixing roles. For example, evaluation can prompt the parties to become more adversarial in an effort to sway the mediator. The mediator's evaluation can steal the focus from party responsibility for creative problem-solving. And there is little protection from an incorrect mediator evaluation; while the parties are not bound by the mediator's opinion, it has the potential to profoundly impact bargaining power.

Nonetheless, in situations where both parties want the mediator's opinion, and the mediation is effectively at an impasse, the mediator might consider "switching hats" and giving expert advice. Before doing that, though, the mediator should warn the parties that her ability to assist as a mediator might be negatively impacted after she gives an opinion that will certainly disfavor one party and that her opinion is based on information that is different than what a judge or arbiter would hear (assuming some of the mediation has been conducted in caucuses where information was shared that could not be rebutted by the other party).

If the parties give their informed consent to the mediator switching roles, then the mediator can proceed, provided she has the necessary credentials to give the requested advice and she follows appropriate practice and ethical guidelines for rendering that service.

20. Should a mediator let one party pay her entire mediator fee?

If possible, no. The danger is obvious: if only one party pays the mediator's fee, the mediator's representation that she is neutral can be compromised. The practice of having each party pay 50% of the mediator's fee avoids that problem.

The practical difficulty is that one party is typically willing and able to pay the mediator's fee and, unless it does so, the other party might not be able to afford to participate. In recent years, for example, the practice has developed that the mediator's entire fee for those handling cases involving litigants in employment discrimination cases or persons involved in personal injury litigation is paid for by the employer and insurance company respectively. Party representatives are comfortable with this practice and confident that it does not undermine the mediator's role. It is, however, worrisome, for it might generate public skepticism about a mediator's proclaimed neutrality. While persons always need to be open to considering multiple models for financing mediation services, a mediator has an ethical duty to make certain her fee arrangements do not adversely impact her ability to conduct a mediation in an impartial, neutral manner nor undermine confidence in the integrity of the process she is conducting.

14

Conclusion

We have spent decades trying to develop "out-of-the-box" thinking. Perhaps the next step is to realize that THERE IS NO BOX.

Amory Loving

We often use mediating skills and strategies even when we are not assuming a mediator's role. When we try to make a sale to a customer, discipline an employee without creating a backlash, conduct a staff meeting, or cajole a child into practicing his musical instrument, we improve our chances of success by systematically considering how and where we will begin the discussion, the order in which we will discuss the topics, and the leverage we can use in trying to persuade someone to accept our proposal. We use private meetings to uncover hidden information and agendas. We seek to make understandings as clear and appealing as they can be. In short, we apply the elements of BADGER. They are useful skills that enable us to cope with life's daily challenges.

As the diversity of examples in this book shows, assuming a mediator's role is an inescapable part of our lives. Whether we are formally appointed to serve as a mediator or the role is informally thrust upon us, we often manage the process of resolving conflict not by deciding how others must act but by prodding them—BADGERing them—into deciding for themselves how they will reconcile their differences. Being a capable mediator is not only important to individuals who want to do it professionally; it is also invaluable to anyone else who wants to resolve differences effectively.

Mediating well is not easy; it is a complex process with many variables. But this multiplicity of factors does not reduce mediating to an art form in which anything one does is acceptable or for which one must have an inborn talent. There are ways to prepare, duties to perform, and a structure to develop; there are options for trying to persuade parties to change their position and procedures for bringing discussions to a close. People can execute these responsibilities brilliantly or ineptly. They can also sharpen their skills in performing these tasks—they can become better at mediating.

Mediating is a rewarding role to play. It is more than just peacekeeping—restraining people from shooting at one another, literally or figuratively. While that is not an insignificant achievement, it is only the beginning. Cities do not become communities simply because there are no riots in the street. Corporations and universities do not become cohesive enterprises merely because colleagues are not operating at cross-purposes. They require a building process as well. A mediator can make a significant contribution to that process of building relationships among individuals, groups, or nations; he can help to structure arrangements that strengthen freedom and creativity, promote communication and trust, and secure dignity.

When people resolve their disputes, they may feel relief, exhilaration and pride. They have accomplished something; they have put something behind them and can get on with their lives. A mediator is not a bystander who merely observes resolutions develop. He is someone who commits his talents to managing a discussion process through which disputants develop understanding and mutual commitments to action. He creates a climate that promotes respect. He generates creative problem-solving. He challenges parties to reach agreement by cooperating with, rather than prevailing over, each other. The final test of the value of mediation comes when people must match their conduct to their rhetoric and put their mediated agreement into play.

When the mediator knows that he has contributed to the success of the process at each of these levels, the joy of mediating is immense.

Recommended for
Further Reading

The following short list might be a reader's next step in a study of mediation. Note that the broader study of conflict resolution, negotiation, and political theory and values is part of the mediator's orientation and foundation. The authors acknowledge their own intellectual debt to the books listed here.

Books on Designing Dispute Resolution Systems

Designing Conflict Management Systems: A Guide to Creating Productive and Healthy Organizations, Costantino & Merchant (Jossey-Bass 1996).
Designing Systems and Processes for Managing Disputes, Rogers, Bordone, Sander, and McEwen (2012).
Getting Disputes Resolved: Designing Systems to Cut the Costs of Conflict, Goldberg, Brett & Ury (Jossey-Bass 1988).

Books on Negotiation

A Behavioral Theory of Labor Negotiations: An Analysis of a Social Interaction System, Walton & McKersie (2nd ed., ILR Press 1991).
Bargaining for Advantage: Negotiation Strategies for Reasonable People, Shell (2nd ed., Penguin 2006).
Beyond Winning: Negotiating to Create Value in Deals and Disputes, Mnookin, Peppet & Tulumello (Belknap Press 2000).
Getting Past No: Negotiating with Difficult People, Ury (Bantam Books 1991).
Getting to Yes: Negotiating Agreement Without Giving In, Fisher, Ury & Patton (Penguin 3rd ed., 2011).
Rethinking Negotiation Teaching (4 volumes), Christopher Honeyman, James Coben, and Giuseppe DePalo, eds. (DRI Press: 2009, 2010, 2012, 2013).
The Manager as Negotiator: Bargaining for Cooperation and Competitive Gain, Lax & Sebenius (The Free Press 1986).

Books on Mediation

Managing Public Disputes: A Practical Guide for Government, Business, and Citizens' Groups, Carpenter & Kennedy (2nd ed., Jossey-Bass 2001).

Mediating Legal Disputes: Effective Strategies for Lawyers and Mediators, Golann (Aspen Law and Business 1996).

Stories Mediators Tell, Eric Galton and Lela Love, eds. (ABA Publishing 2012).

Techniques of Mediation in Labor Disputes, Maggiolo (Oceana Publications 1971).

The Fundamentals of Family Mediation, Haynes (State University of New York Press 1994).

The Mediation Process, Christopher Moore (Jossey-Bass 2003).

The Promise of Mediation: The Transformative Approach to Conflict, Bush & Folger (revised ed., Jossey-Bass 2005).

When Talk Works: Profiles of Mediators, Kolb & Associates (Jossey-Bass 1994).

Law School Textbooks on Mediation

(include history, law, policy, ethics and codes of conduct)

Mediation: Practice, Policy and Ethics, Menkel-Meadow, Love & Schneider (Aspen 2006).

Mediation Theory and Practice, Alfini, Press & Stulberg (Lexis Publishing 3rd ed. 2013).

Books on Political Theory and Values

Anarchy, State and Utopia, Nozick (Basic Books 1974).

On Liberty, Mill (Bantam Books 1993).

Political Liberalism, Rawls (Columbia University Press 1993).

When the People Speak: Deliberative Democracy and Public Consultation, Fishkin (Oxford University Press 2009).

Appendix

Model Standards of Conduct for Mediators

AMERICAN ARBITRATION ASSOCIATION
(ADOPTED SEPTEMBER 8, 2005)

AMERICAN BAR ASSOCIATION
(ADOPTED AUGUST 9, 2005)

ASSOCIATION FOR CONFLICT RESOLUTION
(ADOPTED AUGUST 22, 2005)

SEPTEMBER 2005

The Model Standards of Conduct for Mediators
September 2005

The *Model Standards of Conduct for Mediators* was prepared in 1994 by the American Arbitration Association, the American Bar Association's Section of Dispute Resolution, and the Association for Conflict Resolution.[1] A joint committee consisting of representatives from the same successor organizations revised the Model Standards in 2005.[2] Both the original 1994 version and the 2005 revision have been approved by each participating organization.

---

1. The Association for Conflict Resolution is a merged organization of the Academy of Family Mediators, the Conflict Resolution Education Network and the Society of Professionals in Dispute Resolution (SPIDR). SPIDR was the third participating organization in the development of the 1994 Standards.

2. Reporter's Notes, which are not part of these Standards and therefore have not been specifically approved by any of the organizations, provide commentary regarding these revisions.

Preamble

Mediation is used to resolve a broad range of conflicts within a variety of settings. These Standards are designed to serve as fundamental ethical guidelines for persons mediating in all practice contexts. They serve three primary goals: to guide the conduct of mediators; to inform the mediating parties; and to promote public confidence in mediation as a process for resolving disputes.

Mediation is a process in which an impartial third party facilitates communication and negotiation and promotes voluntary decision making by the parties to the dispute.

Mediation serves various purposes, including providing the opportunity for parties to define and clarify issues, understand different perspectives, identify interests, explore and assess possible solutions, and reach mutually satisfactory agreements, when desired.

Note on Construction

These Standards are to be read and construed in their entirety. There is no priority significance attached to the sequence in which the Standards appear.

The use of the term "shall" in a Standard indicates that the mediator must follow the practice described. The use of the term "should" indicates that the practice described in the standard is highly desirable, but not required, and is to be departed from only for very strong reasons and requires careful use of judgment and discretion.

The use of the term "mediator" is understood to be inclusive so that it applies to co-mediator models.

> These Standards do not include specific temporal parameters when referencing a mediation, and therefore, do not define the exact beginning or ending of a mediation.

Various aspects of a mediation, including some matters covered by these Standards, may also be affected by applicable law, court rules, regulations, other applicable professional rules, mediation rules to which the parties have agreed and other agreements of the parties. These sources may create conflicts with, and may take precedence over, these Standards. However, a mediator should make every effort to comply with the spirit and intent of these Standards in resolving such conflicts. This effort should include honoring all remaining Standards not in conflict with these other sources.

These Standards, unless and until adopted by a court or other regulatory authority do not have the force of law. Nonetheless, the fact that these Standards have been adopted by the respective sponsoring entities, should alert media-tors to the fact that the Standards might be viewed as establishing a standard of care for mediators.

STANDARD I. SELF-DETERMINATION

A. A mediator shall conduct a mediation based on the principle of party self-determination. Self-determination is the act of coming to a voluntary, un-coerced decision in which each party makes free and informed choices as to process and outcome. Parties may exercise self-determination at any stage of a mediation, including mediator selection, process design, par-ticipation in or withdrawal from the process, and outcomes.

   1. Although party self-determination for process design is a fundamen-tal principle of mediation practice, a mediator may need to balance such party self-determination with a mediator's duty to conduct a quality process in accordance with these Standards.

   2. A mediator cannot personally ensure that each party has made free and informed choices to reach particular decisions, but, where ap-propriate, a mediator should make the parties aware of the impor-tance of consulting other professionals to help them make informed choices.

B. A mediator shall not undermine party self-determination by any party for reasons such as higher settlement rates, egos, increased fees, or outside pressures from court personnel, program administrators, provider or-ganizations, the media or others.

STANDARD II. IMPARTIALITY

A. A mediator shall decline a mediation if the mediator cannot conduct it in an impartial manner. Impartiality means freedom from favoritism, bias or prejudice.

B. A mediator shall conduct a mediation in an impartial manner and avoid conduct that gives the appearance of partiality.

   1. A mediator should not act with partiality or prejudice based on any participant's personal characteristics, background, values and beliefs, or performance at a mediation, or any other reason.

   2. A mediator should neither give nor accept a gift, favor, loan or other item of value that raises a question as to the mediator's actual or per-ceived impartiality.

   3. A mediator may accept or give de minimis gifts or incidental items or services that are provided to facilitate a mediation or respect cultural norms so long as such practices do not raise questions as to a media-tor's actual or perceived impartiality.

C. If at any time a mediator is unable to conduct a mediation in an impartial manner, the mediator shall withdraw.

STANDARD III. CONFLICTS OF INTEREST

A. A mediator shall avoid a conflict of interest or the appearance of a conflict of interest during and after a mediation. A conflict of interest can arise from involvement by a mediator with the subject matter of the dispute or from any relationship between a mediator and any mediation participant, whether past or present, personal or professional, that reasonably raises a question of a mediator's impartiality.

B. A mediator shall make a reasonable inquiry to determine whether there are any facts that a reasonable individual would consider likely to create a potential or actual conflict of interest for a mediator. A mediator's actions necessary to accomplish a reasonable inquiry into potential conflicts of interest may vary based on practice context.

C. A mediator shall disclose, as soon as practicable, all actual and potential conflicts of interest that are reasonably known to the mediator and could reasonably be seen as raising a question about the mediator's impartiality. After disclosure, if all parties agree, the mediator may proceed with the mediation.

D. If a mediator learns any fact after accepting a mediation that raises a question with respect to that mediator's service creating a potential or actual conflict of interest, the mediator shall disclose it as quickly as practicable. After disclosure, if all parties agree, the mediator may proceed with the mediation.

E. If a mediator's conflict of interest might reasonably be viewed as undermining the integrity of the mediation, a mediator shall withdraw from or decline to proceed with the mediation regardless of the expressed desire or agreement of the parties to the contrary.

F. Subsequent to a mediation, a mediator shall not establish another relationship with any of the participants in any matter that would raise questions about the integrity of the mediation. When a mediator develops personal or professional relationships with parties, other individuals or organizations following a mediation in which they were involved, the mediator should consider factors such as time elapsed following the mediation, the nature of the relationships established, and services offered when determining whether the relationships might create a perceived or actual conflict of interest.

STANDARD IV. COMPETENCE

A. A mediator shall mediate only when the mediator has the necessary competence to satisfy the reasonable expectations of the parties.

1. Any person may be selected as a mediator, provided that the parties are satisfied with the mediator's competence and qualifications. Train-

ing, experience in mediation, skills, cultural understandings and other qualities are often necessary for mediator competence. A person who offers to serve as a mediator creates the expectation that the person is competent to mediate effectively.

2. A mediator should attend educational programs and related activities to maintain and enhance the mediator's knowledge and skills related to mediation.

3. A mediator should have available for the parties' information relevant to the mediator's training, education, experience and approach to conducting a mediation.

B. If a mediator, during the course of a mediation determines that the mediator cannot conduct the mediation competently, the mediator shall discuss that determination with the parties as soon as is practicable and take appropriate steps to address the situation, including, but not limited to, withdrawing or requesting appropriate assistance.

C. If a mediator's ability to conduct a mediation is impaired by drugs, alcohol, medication or otherwise, the mediator shall not conduct the mediation.

STANDARD V. CONFIDENTIALITY

A. A mediator shall maintain the confidentiality of all information obtained by the mediator in mediation, unless otherwise agreed to by the parties or required by applicable law.

1. If the parties to a mediation agree that the mediator may disclose information obtained during the mediation, the mediator may do so.

2. A mediator should not communicate to any non-participant information about how the parties acted in the mediation. A mediator may report, if required, whether parties appeared at a scheduled mediation and whether or not the parties reached a resolution.

3. If a mediator participates in teaching, research or evaluation of mediation, the mediator should protect the anonymity of the parties and abide by their reasonable expectations regarding confidentiality.

B. A mediator who meets with any persons in private session during a mediation shall not convey directly or indirectly to any other person, any information that was obtained during that private session without the consent of the disclosing person.

C. A mediator shall promote understanding among the parties of the extent to which the parties will maintain confidentiality of information they obtain in a mediation.

D. Depending on the circumstance of a mediation, the parties may have varying expectations regarding confidentiality that a mediator should address.

The parties may make their own rules with respect to confidentiality, or the accepted practice of an individual mediator or institution may dictate a particular set of expectations.

STANDARD VI. QUALITY OF THE PROCESS

A. A mediator shall conduct a mediation in accordance with these Standards and in a manner that promotes diligence, timeliness, safety, presence of the appropriate participants, party participation, procedural fairness, party competency and mutual respect among all participants.

1. A mediator should agree to mediate only when the mediator is prepared to commit the attention essential to an effective mediation.

2. A mediator should only accept cases when the mediator can satisfy the reasonable expectation of the parties concerning the timing of a mediation.

3. The presence or absence of persons at a mediation depends on the agreement of the parties and the mediator. The parties and mediator may agree that others may be excluded from particular sessions or from all sessions.

4. A mediator should promote honesty and candor between and among all participants, and a mediator shall not knowingly misrepresent any material fact or circumstance in the course of a mediation.

5. The role of a mediator differs substantially from other professional roles. Mixing the role of a mediator and the role of another profession is problematic and thus, a mediator should distinguish between the roles. A mediator may provide information that the mediator is qualified by training or experience to provide, only if the mediator can do so consistent with these Standards.

6. A mediator shall not conduct a dispute resolution procedure other than mediation but label it mediation in an effort to gain the protection of rules, statutes, or other governing authorities pertaining to mediation.

7. A mediator may recommend, when appropriate, that parties consider resolving their dispute through arbitration, counseling, neutral evaluation or other processes.

8. A mediator shall not undertake an additional dispute resolution role in the same matter without the consent of the parties. Before providing such service, a mediator shall inform the parties of the implications of the change in process and obtain their consent to the change. A mediator who undertakes such role assumes different duties and responsibilities that may be governed by other standards.

9. If a mediation is being used to further criminal conduct, a mediator should take appropriate steps including, if necessary, postponing, withdrawing from or terminating the mediation.

10. If a party appears to have difficulty comprehending the process, issues, or settlement options, or difficulty participating in a mediation, the mediator should explore the circumstances and potential accommodations, modifications or adjustments that would make possible the party's capacity to comprehend, participate and exercise self-determination.

B. If a mediator is made aware of domestic abuse or violence among the parties, the mediator shall take appropriate steps including, if necessary, postponing, withdrawing from or terminating the mediation.

C. If a mediator believes that participant conduct, including that of the mediator, jeopardizes conducting a mediation consistent with these Standards, a mediator shall take appropriate steps including, if necessary, postponing, withdrawing from or terminating the mediation.

STANDARD VII. ADVERTISING AND SOLICITATION

A. A mediator shall be truthful and not misleading when advertising, soliciting or otherwise communicating the mediator's qualifications, experience, services and fees.

1. A mediator should not include any promises as to outcome in communications, including business cards, stationery, or computer-based communications.

2. A mediator should only claim to meet the mediator qualifications of a governmental entity or private organization if that entity or organization has a recognized procedure for qualifying mediators and it grants such status to the mediator.

B. A mediator shall not solicit in a manner that gives an appearance of partiality for or against a party or otherwise undermines the integrity of the process.

C. A mediator shall not communicate to others, in promotional materials or through other forms of communication, the names of persons served without their permission.

STANDARD VIII. FEES AND OTHER CHARGES

A. A mediator shall provide each party or each party's representative true and complete information about mediation fees, expenses and any other actual or potential charges that may be incurred in connection with a mediation.

1. If a mediator charges fees, the mediator should develop them in light of all relevant factors, including the type and complexity of the mat-

ter, the qualifications of the mediator, the time required and the rates customary for such mediation services.

   2. A mediator's fee arrangement should be in writing unless the parties request otherwise.

B. A mediator shall not charge fees in a manner that impairs a mediator's impartiality.

   1. A mediator should not enter into a fee agreement which is contingent upon the result of the mediation or amount of the settlement.

   2. While a mediator may accept unequal fee payments from the parties, a mediator should not use fee arrangements that adversely impact the mediator's ability to conduct a mediation in an impartial manner.

STANDARD IX. ADVANCEMENT OF MEDIATION PRACTICE

A. A mediator should act in a manner that advances the practice of mediation. A mediator promotes this Standard by engaging in some or all of the following:

   1. Fostering diversity within the field of mediation.

   2. Striving to make mediation accessible to those who elect to use it, including providing services at a reduced rate or on a pro bono basis as appropriate.

   3. Participating in research when given the opportunity, including obtaining participant feedback when appropriate.

   4. Participating in outreach and education efforts to assist the public in developing an improved understanding of, and appreciation for, mediation.

   5. Assisting newer mediators through training, mentoring and networking.

B. A mediator should demonstrate respect for differing points of view within the field, seek to learn from other mediators and work together with other mediators to improve the profession and better serve people in conflict.

About the Authors

Joseph (Josh) B. Stulberg and **Lela P. Love** have worked as a mediation training team for more than twenty five years, designing and delivering programs throughout the United States and abroad. They have also collaborated on a variety of writing projects for law journals and books.

Josh is the Michael E. Moritz Chair in Alternative Dispute Resolution at The Ohio State University Moritz College of Law where he teaches its multi-party mediation clinic, legal negotiation, and jurisprudence. An active mediator and arbitrator of labor, commercial, construction, family, community, and public policy disputes, he has been a mediator trainer since 1973; he has developed model training programs and core curriculum for training mediators to serve in state and federal government mediation programs, community dispute resolution centers, peer mediation projects, and comprehensive court-annexed civil and family mediation initiatives.

A former Vice President of the American Arbitration Association in charge of its Community Dispute Services, Josh has written extensively on conflict resolution.

Josh earned his J.D. degree from New York University School of Law and his Ph.D. in philosophy from the University of Rochester. He is a member of the New York Bar and a Distinguished Fellow of the American College of Civil Trial Mediators. He was one of 18 international scholars to be awarded a 2012 Ikerbasque Research Fellowship.

Lela is a Professor of Law at Benjamin N. Cardozo School of Law, where she developed and directs the Mediation Clinic and Cardozo's Kukin Program for Conflict Resolution. Lela's mediation practice includes trust and estate matters, business, corporate and partnership conflicts, police-civilian cases, discrimination and employment cases, and public policy disputes. She regularly conducts mediation training programs. She has written widely on the topic of mediation and mediated a simulated product liability dispute for COURT TV. She has co-authored three law school textbooks on dispute resolution and co-edited, with Eric Galton, a collection of stories about mediation, *Stories Mediators Tell*. She is past Chair of the American Bar Association Section on

Dispute Resolution. She has received a life-time achievement award from the American College of Civil Trial Mediators and from the International Academy of Mediators.

Prior to moving into the dispute resolution field, Lela developed and directed a Small Business Clinic for George Washington University Law School.

Lela received a B.A. from Harvard University, a M.Ed. from Virginia Commonwealth University and a J.D. degree from Georgetown University Law Center. She is a member of the Bar in New York, New Hampshire and the District of Columbia.